Spring, Summer, Asteroid, Bird

ALSO BY HENRY LIEN

Peasprout Chen,
Future Legend of Skate and Sword

Peasprout Chen:
Battle of Champions

Spring, Summer, Asteroid, Bird

THE ART OF EASTERN STORYTELLING

HENRY LIEN

W. W. NORTON & COMPANY
Independent Publishers Since 1923

For information about permission to reproduce selections from this book, write to
Permissions, W. W. Norton & Company, Inc., 500 Fifth Avenue, New York, NY 10110

For information about special discounts for bulk purchases, please contact W. W. Norton
Special Sales at specialsales@wwnorton.com or 800-233-4830

Manufacturing by Lakeside Book Company
Book design by Daniel Lagin
Production manager: Louise Mattarelliano

ISBN 978-1-324-07910-1 (pbk.)

W. W. Norton & Company, Inc., 500 Fifth Avenue, New York, NY 10110
www.wwnorton.com

W. W. Norton & Company Ltd., 15 Carlisle Street, London W1D 3BS

10 9 8 7 6 5 4 3 2 1

I devote this book to my birds and to Hayao Miyazaki.

CONTENTS

OPENING BOWS

Diversity = Forms, Not Just Faces...3

A Game of Lenses...4

Disclaimers and Definitions...7

Hamilton and Different Levels of Diversity....................................8

Cultural Appropriation..9

"Spring, Summer, Asteroid, Bird"..11

ACT ONE—The East Asian Four-Act Story Structure

Western Story Structures...17

East Asian Four-Act Structure..21

"The Daughters of Itoya"...25

Parasite..29

Nintendo (*Mario* and *Zelda* Games)..39

Hard-Boiled Wonderland and the End of the World......................46

Your Name..53

Four-Act Structure in Western Stories...61

ACT TWO—Circular/Nested Story Structures

Circular/Nested Structures...69

The Story of the Stone...72

Rashomon...75

The Merchant and the Alchemist's Gate.....................................81

Everything Everywhere All at Once...88

Metroid Games...94

Circular/Nested Structures in Western Stories..............................97

ACT THREE—People Aren't People

Introduction—"Shakespeare in the Bush"..103

Cultural Arrogance..105

Individualism versus Collectivism...107

Surface Diversity...113

The Opposite of Surface Diversity..115

ACT FOUR—Values Dictate Structures

Values Dictate Structures...123

Values Dictating Four-Act Structure..125

My Neighbor Totoro..127

Values Dictating Circular/Nested Structures..134

Hero...139

The Thousand and One Nights..147

CLOSING BOWS

APPENDIX: Activities

Questions for Readers...163

Questions for Writers...167

Acknowledgments...173

Notes..175

Opening Bows

DIVERSITY = FORMS, NOT JUST FACES

Early twenty-first-century dialogue in the West around diversity in the arts tends to focus on the identities of characters, creators, and performers. As important as that is, diversity can be about more than just plopping different faces into stories that are 100 percent Western in spirit. It can and should also encompass diverse story structures from non-Western traditions and the themes and values that inform them. Just as values are not universal across all cultures, the shape of a satisfying story is not limited to one model either.

This book examines how elements that we consider storytelling staples in the West, such as the three-act story structure and a focus on an individual's development, are far from representative of all storytelling traditions. It introduces readers to what can constitute satisfying structures in Eastern storytelling and explores how they differ radically from Western structures because their underlying values differ.

Throughout the book, I use examples from books, films, and video games, and I often include detailed summaries of their plots. As a result, the book teems with plot spoilers. The ideal way to read this book is to read, watch, or play each work discussed before reading the section analyzing that work. Spoilerphobes are hereby warned that the book contains extensive and explicit instances of plot nudity.

A GAME OF LENSES

Let's play a game. I'm going to use a very traditional Chinese/Taiwanese lens to describe four popular books that are well known here in the exotic Occident. Guess the book (titles written backward).

Q. Majestic gold dragon is murdered by band of thieves and homeless men.

A. *Tibboh eht (Neiklot R. R. J)*

Let's autopsy that a bit. In the Western telling, the protagonist Bilbo and a band of dwarves go on a quest to steal back treasure from a malevolent dragon. However, in Chinese/Taiwanese culture, the dragon is revered as divine, wise, benevolent, and powerful, but peaceful. Any story in which a dragon is killed is automatically a tragedy. Further, in a traditional and conservative society, Bilbo and the dwarves would be considered thieves and homeless men. Such elements would be viewed as failed citizens and parasites on society. A story in which such characters triumph is going to be received as dark and wrong.

Q. Only daughter receives propitious offer of marriage from rich older man.

A. *Thgiliwt (Reyem Einehpets)*

Okay, so I cheated a bit there, as Edward Cullen, the vampire love interest of the protagonist, is a *significantly* older man. But I'm making the point that vampires don't exist in Chinese/Taiwanese lore. Thus, any downsides of vampirism in a potential son-in-law would sail right over the heads of traditional Chinese/Taiwanese parents.

Q. Harmony is preserved in the empire through athletics.
A. *Semag Regnuh Eht (Snilloc Ennazus)*

In the Western telling, the government's yearly televised sporting event, in which children fight to the death, is seen as tyrannical. If we unpack this story concept while wearing a pair of traditional Chinese cultural lenses, we're assessing it from the viewpoint of a society that values order and is wary of separatist provinces and ethnic minorities stirring unrest. Any activity that keeps the populace subjugated, especially one that directs potentially troublesome energy into something as wholesome as athletics, would be seen as a superb idea.

Note that the story might be read very differently through a Taiwanese lens, even a very traditional one, given the history and culture of Taiwan and China's belief that Taiwan is a renegade province. In fact, the three-fingered salute from the film adaptation of the book series has been adopted by pro-democracy protesters who are resisting autocratic and authoritarian rule in countries such as Thailand and Myanmar.

Q. One daughter marries the richest boy in her village, two marry paupers, the fourth ends up dead.
A. *Nemow Elttil (Ttocla Yam Asiuol)*

Seen through a Western lens, this book tells the poignant story of four women who experience the joys and sorrows of life. But again, if we're viewing this through a traditional Chinese/Taiwanese lens, we're looking at a family that has no sons, has four daughters, is no longer rich, and is of high-enough station that it would be a debasement for the daughters to seek most of the types of work available to women. In short, we're looking at a family careening toward generational decline. Traditional readers would be most concerned with whom the daughters marry and how they fare socially, not the daughters' individual self-actualization.

Further, the author of the book took care to show the beauty of Beth's life. Though short and seemingly small in scope, Beth's life was filled with meaning that arose from her quietly but steadily living according to her values. Traditional Chinese/Taiwanese culture is deeply superstitious and neurotically fearful of death. People avoid saying the number "four" because it sounds too close to the word for death. Buildings are built without fourth floors because no one would want to rent on the death floor. Thus, the idea of a life cut short would be a hard sell as a thing of beauty. It would be at best a tragedy and at worst a taint on the whole family.

Further, Beth's story unintentionally reinforces the idea that girls should stay at home. Beth went outside once, caught a disease from some German babies, and *died*. In short, the beauty of Beth's life would be mutilated beyond recognition in cultural translation.

The point of this game is to show (a) how vastly different cultural values can be; (b) how those values serve as lenses that alter what is viewed as a satisfying story in a given culture; and (c) how true diversity in the arts should encompass diverse story forms and themes, in addition to diverse faces.

DISCLAIMERS AND DEFINITIONS

This book is not a value judgment on the superiority of Western or Eastern storytelling; a formula for creating Eastern stories; an academic treatise; an anthropological study; an ethnological study; a sociological study; or an authoritative or definitive statement on anything. Rather, it is an x-ray of one working author's own attempts to make sense of things he's observed and can't get out of his head.

Also, a note about definitions. I fling around terms like "the West" and "Western." Obviously, "the West" is not a monolith, and many races, ethnicities, religions, identities, cultures, traditions, and nations are located geographically in the West. When I use those terms, I am referring to the dominant, canonical culture in places such as Europe and North America, which is derived from European culture.

Finally, I wish to state in the firmest way possible that the concepts I examine in this book are not rigidly absolute or mutually exclusive. "Western storytelling" and "Eastern storytelling" are not legally, scientifically, or divinely defined. Their borders are porous. Of course there are Western stories that aren't told in the three-act structure and Eastern stories that are. There are Eastern stories that are about individual heroism and Western stories that aren't. I struggle to find words to express sufficient disapproval of the impulse to reduce these ideas to black and white. This book examines and makes observations on stories that exist along a living spectrum, not within an ossified binary.

HAMILTON AND DIFFERENT LEVELS OF DIVERSITY

The discussion around the Tony Award– and Pulitzer Prize–winning musical *Hamilton* is a good case study in the different levels on which diversity can operate. The musical, created by Puerto Rican playwright Lin-Manuel Miranda, is about American revolutionary and Founding Father Alexander Hamilton. It features actors of color portraying iconic White American historical figures, and it uses hip-hop, a medium created by Black Americans, to tell its story. For these reasons, the musical has been praised as embracing diversity, but it has also been criticized by some for engaging in "surface" diversity by employing a diverse cast but still choosing to tell a story entirely *about* White people.

In fact, though, the use of hip-hop as the vehicle for *Hamilton*'s story, which is integral to the musical's personality and uniqueness, speaks to the fact that diversity in storytelling can operate on many different levels. Leslie Odom Jr., who originated the role of Aaron Burr in *Hamilton*, said in the *New York Times* that the significance of the play was related not only to "who has the mic, who is allowed to tell the story" but also to "what language the story is told in."[1] In other words, the actual form of the telling, rather than just the characters or subject matter of the story, is how *Hamilton* embraces diversity. It is analogous to how a Kabuki retelling of King Arthur or a Bollywood interpretation of *Romeo and Juliet* would be considered diverse, even though the characters in the stories of King Arthur and *Romeo and Juliet* are almost exclusively White. Diversity encompasses artistic forms, not just faces and names.

CULTURAL APPROPRIATION

In my opinion, the study or practice of Eastern storytelling forms and themes does not in itself constitute cultural appropriation, regardless of the background or lived experience of the student or practitioner.

I define "cultural appropriation" as more than just the practice of taking ideas from another culture. Rather, it's the practice of selectively or randomly using cosmetic aspects of the culture while failing to appreciate the larger cultural context from which they came. It's a form of cosplay that plucks superficial and trivial elements of a culture while failing to understand and honor core differences in values, aesthetics, or spirit and how those elements can radically change what constitutes satisfying story forms and themes. It's the animated musical with a main character (usually female) from some non-Western culture in a non-Western setting nonetheless talking and acting exactly like an American teenager, defying their parents, running into the ocean, singing an "I Want" song, and launching into a three-act story to "find themselves" and "own their power." That's not diversity. That's a Western story in non-Western drag. *That*'s cultural appropriation.

On the other hand, learning about how Eastern storytelling traditions are fundamentally different from Western storytelling traditions doesn't constitute superficial, trivial adoption of cosmetic elements and thus is not cultural appropriation. In fact, it is in some meaningful way the very opposite of cultural appropriation.

Note that I have no interest in serving as the cultural appropriation police. We all have our guilty favorites. I admit to loving the film version of *Memoirs of a Geisha*, especially its beautifully constructed script by Robin Swicord. I also don't use the film to learn about actual geisha culture (I would recommend instead *Geisha, A Life* by Mineko Iwasaki). I also realize that a film with Chinese actresses playing Japanese geisha speaking in English is about as accurate as a film with French actresses playing German princesses all speaking Russian. So I'm not here to enforce any sort of cultural purity. I am here though to advocate for being honest about what's a guilty pleasure and what's a meaningful exploration of a culture.

"SPRING, SUMMER, ASTEROID, BIRD"

Before we punch the red button and launch into actual exploration of Eastern storytelling, I need to tell you a story entitled "Spring, Summer, Asteroid, Bird." This is a true story, although the names are fictitious.

····

It was a lazy spring afternoon in southern Montana. Chelsea was sitting on the branch of a fig tree at the edge of the dense forest. As she breathed in the tree's sickly sweet, mock-rot scent, she kept an eye on Marilyn, her cousin many times removed. She didn't trust Marilyn. Marilyn hadn't ever actually done anything wrong to Chelsea. Chelsea just judged Marilyn based on how she looked. But it was all right, because Marilyn was super judgy about looks as well.

Marilyn wasn't thinking about Chelsea that spring afternoon, though. She was busy circling the floodplains, searching for herbivores to eat and avoiding the other local tyrannosaurs. Marilyn didn't hate her tiny cousin Chelsea. She simply didn't register that Chelsea existed. A thing as small as Chelsea mattered no more to a statuesque tyrannosaur hen like Marilyn than a fly or fern did.

Thus, Marilyn remained oblivious when little Chelsea laid her first clutch of eggs that summer in the sickly-sweet fig tree. Chelsea fed her hatchlings the tree's seed-packed fruit, which were abundant, convenient, and tasty. Marilyn liked that tree too because its mock-rot scent appealed to her scavenger side. Marilyn would rub against it to uncase her pin feathers and cover herself in the scent. Marilyn thought it was pretty ludicrous that her pathetic little cousin put on so hysterical a performance of flapping and peeping each time Marilyn scratched herself against the trunk of the tree. As if Marilyn cared anything about Chelsea and her babies; as if things that had no teeth and ate fruit and seeds were worth noticing.

I fly above the fig tree, but Chelsea cannot see me, not even when the late summer breeze momentarily parts the leaves, baring her nest to the open sky. That is because I am thirty-one million miles above her head. My destiny is to be a mass murderer, the greatest single mass murderer in the history of the Earth. I do not know that, however, because I do not know about a planet called Earth, because I have never been there. It is also because I cannot know anything, since I am a six-mile-wide chunk of rock, or else ice and dust. I am not sure because I have no mind.

When I strike the Gulf of Mexico, traveling at fifty-six thousand miles per hour, I impact with the force of ten billion Hiroshima bombs. I am vaporized but not forgotten. I push the earth down almost nineteen miles. My remains form a mushroom cloud hundreds of miles high and wide. The heat travels almost one thousand miles from the impact epicenter, torching everything. Chelsea's fig tree is more than one thousand miles away, so it survives the initial impact. However, hot rocks thrown up by the impact shower back down on the Earth, lighting forest fires across the planet, which eventually reach the dense forests circling the floodplains in Montana. The dust cloud travels around the globe in just a few hours. I create magnitude 10 or 11 earthquakes, which are ten to one hundred times more powerful than any that have shaken this planet before. The forest fires burn for up to two years. Their smoke joins the ejected rock and smoke from the impact to form a dirty cloud that blocks out sunlight for years more. Ecosystems quickly collapse. Plants die, which starves herbivores, which in turn starves carnivores. The larger they are, the more quickly they starve.

Chelsea pecked at the ground, below the remains of the very fig tree from which she had watched her cousin Marilyn and laid her first clutch of eggs. The tree no longer had a sickly-sweet aroma, as it was dead. The rot in the air was not a mock smell—there were plenty of piles of real decay punctuating the blasted landscape. Chelsea located a seed, perhaps one that had tiny generations of fig trees inside it, and swallowed the nutrient-rich package. In the years since the Darkening and the heat and the cold that followed, every dinosaur that required teeth to eat died. Seeds did not require teeth. They seemed made for beaks to find and shell. Her towering, toothed cousins had no ability to eat all the nutritive seeds lying on the ground. And seeds survived cold and heat and stayed edible for years. Chelsea found another seed, worked it with her beak, and deftly shelled it. When she had filled her crop, she flew back to her nest. Her clutch of newly hatched dinosaurs peeped for warm, shelled seeds, aiming their yawning beaks to her, like flowers to a sun they had never seen.

One day, Chelsea died. Sixty-five million years passed. However, her DNA remains. It could be in any climate. On any continent. She and her fellow beaked, seed-eating dinosaurs are now the most populous species on Earth. Some of them enjoy sitting and building nests in fig trees and inhaling their sickly-sweet scent.

A handful of the skeletons of her cousin Marilyn's side of the family turned to stone and their bones were connected in museums, sometimes in embarrassingly wrong postures. Some of the risen mammals believed that the remains of the rest of Marilyn's side of the family were turned into fuel for vehicles that again clouded the Earth's skies, plastic bags that choked the Earth's seas, and plastic dinosaurs that the mammalian young played with and abused. These beliefs, even if untrue, stripped Marilyn and her side of the family of their last dwindling glimmer of dignity. Chelsea could not smile because she was dead, and because she had a beak, but if she could . . .

····

What just happened here?

You were exposed to a story that simultaneously demonstrates two of the structures we will be exploring in this book: the East Asian four-act structure and the circular structure.

Welcome to Eastern storytelling.

Please extend your arms as your safety harness lowers. Enjoy the ride.

ACT ONE

The East Asian Four-
Act Story Structure

WESTERN STORY STRUCTURES

This book won't go into the Western three-act story structure (or the similar five-act Freytag Pyramid variant) in detail. This story structure is currently a popular feature of traditional Western storytelling. However, before we can appreciate how different the East Asian four-act story structure is, we need to sync our understandings of the Western structure.

First, let's x-ray the original *Star Wars: Episode IV—A New Hope* as a specimen of the three-act structure:

ACT ONE—Setup

The main elements are introduced: the Empire, the rebellion, the protagonist (Luke Skywalker), the antagonist (Darth Vader), and so on. The central question is whether the Rebellion will get the architectural plans hidden inside R2-D2 to foil the Empire's new superweapon, the Death Star. Luke gets embroiled in the Rebellion's effort with the help of his teacher, Obi-Wan Kenobi.

ACT TWO—Confrontation

Hurdles are thrown in the way of the main mission: Luke gets trapped on the Death Star, and Darth Vader kills Obi-Wan Kenobi.

ACT THREE—Resolution

Darth Vader fails to kill Luke, and Luke brings the architectural plans to the Rebellion and blows up the Death Star.

The Western three-act story structure and the five-act Freytag Pyramid variant are (a) based on tension, conflict, and resolution; and (b) symmetrical in shape (ascent, climax, descent, plus a central question posed in the first act that is answered in the last act).

The focus on tension, conflict, and resolution exerts pressure on stories to organize their particles into force and opposing force. This funnels stories into a beam aimed at encountering obstacles and overcoming obstacles, which often ends up being about destroying obstacles.

The preference for symmetry is even more defining in Western storytelling. Symmetry does not mean that the three (or five) acts must be of similar length in page count or run time. In fact, in many three-act stories, act two is as long as acts one and three put together. What it means is that the elements found at the beginning of the story should be the same elements found at the end of the story. Western audiences don't want Darth Vader to suddenly appear for the first time in the final act of *Star Wars: Episode IV—A New Hope*. Neither do they want Darth Vader to appear in the first act and then disappear forever from the story. Fundamental elements such as protagonist, antagonist, and central issue or problem should generally appear throughout the story, and certainly in the first and final acts. If a primary element appears in the first act but does not reappear in the final act, then Western audiences will cry, "But you didn't finish the story!" If a primary element doesn't appear in the first act but appears suddenly in the final act, Western audiences will howl, "But that came out of nowhere, and not in a good way!"

Note that the "coming out of nowhere" element used to be considered a feature, not a bug, in ancient Greek drama, a practice called deus ex machina, which translates to "god out of the machine." An otherwise unsolvable plot problem would be solved by the end by a god or goddess entering the story for the first time at the ending. The deity would swoop in to intervene, right wrongs, or otherwise finish the story and rescue it from the corner into which it had painted itself. In ancient stage productions, the actor playing the deity would often enter the stage via a crane or other mechanical device, hence the phrase "god out of the machine." Over time, however, that plot device fell out of favor, and most contemporary Western audiences would recoil at such a plot resolution. We see this in the revulsion that meets endings that rely on the "It was all just a dream" trope.

Thus, tension, conflict, resolution, and symmetry are considered staples of storytelling in Western cultures. I don't think that cultural conditioning is entirely responsible for why stories with these elements feel nourishing. We are wired as a species for pattern recognition. We learn from stories where others of our species meet obstacles and overcome them. They map a sense of order onto a bewildering and dangerous world and serve to pass on ancestral survival tips.

Stories of a hero facing a central problem and persevering and triumphing over challenges and doubts invoke what psychiatrist Carl Jung considered to be archetypes universal to all humanity:

> In each of these images there is a little piece of human psychology and human fate, a remnant of the joys and sorrows that have been repeated countless times in our ancestral history, and on the average follow ever the same course. . . . The moment when this mythological situation reappears is always characterized by a peculiar emotional intensity; it is as though chords in us were struck that had never resounded before. . . . At such moments we are no longer individuals, but the race; the voice of all mankind resounds in us. . . . The impact of an archetype . . . stirs us because it summons up a voice that is stronger than our own. Whoever speaks in primordial images speaks with a thousand voices. . . . He transmutes our personal destiny into the destiny of mankind, and evokes in

us all those beneficent forces that ever and anon have enabled humanity to find a refuge from every peril and to outlive the longest night. That is the secret of great art, and of its effect upon us.[2]

However, even if there are basic elements that are universally nutritive to humankind, storytelling tastes are like dietary tastes. Food the world over might serve the same functions and deliver similar nutrients, but what constitutes a satisfying meal differs from culture to culture, and those tastes are learned and transmitted.

EAST ASIAN FOUR-ACT STRUCTURE

Reader, I introduce you to the East Asian four-act structure. Actually, you probably have met before. Maybe you've even had a memorable evening together. But it was one of those evenings where names were not learned.

The four-act structure is common in China, Japan, Korea, and Taiwan. It is most commonly referred to in the West by its Japanese name, *kishōtenketsu.*

Its most prominent feature is a third-act twist that disrupts the orderly progression of the story and crashes into it like an asteroid. That third-act twist often differs from what we consider a plot twist in Western storytelling because it often introduces an entirely new main character or element. Further, it often changes the very genre of the story, from comedy to thriller, from parlor drama to science fiction.

Other features of the structure include a fourth act that reveals invisible connections among the preceding acts, does not necessarily rely on the defeat of an opponent, and often ends in an abrupt and open manner that encourages lingering contemplation.

As radical as the structure might seem to Western audiences, we will explore in the pages that follow how several popular books, films, and video games have managed to Trojan Horse the structure into Western minds and how the form allows for effects impossible to achieve with other structures.

The four acts are broken down thus:

ACT ONE (KI)—The Introduction of the Main Elements

ACT TWO (SHŌ)—The Development of the Main Elements

ACT THREE (TEN)—The Twist/New Element

ACT FOUR (KETSU)—The Harmonizing of All Elements

The four-act structure is starkly different from Western structures. It is not necessarily based on conflict, tension, and resolution. This does not mean that stories told in the four-act structure are universally devoid of conflict. Remember what I said about resisting the impulse to collapse things into neat binaries. In fact, conflict permeates many of the case studies illustrating the four-act structure that we will examine. What this does mean, though, is that the four-act structure is more interested in exploring the unseen relationships among the story's elements than in pitting them against each other until only one stands.

In addition, the fourth act "harmonizes" all the elements that came before. By "harmonize," I don't necessarily mean a peaceful resolution. I mean that the fourth act contains a revelation about the relationships among the elements that often feels like a new element in itself. This act often ends abruptly and ambiguously, inviting each person to construct their own final understanding of the story that extends beyond the last page or the end credits. This approach offers an opportunity for each person to participate in, personalize, and develop a longer-lasting relationship with the work.

It is also not symmetrical. The first two acts are characterized by a gradual buildup. A radical twist appears in the third act that introduces a new element, late in the story, after the halfway point. (Note, however, that the acts do not have to be uniform in length.) This twist would likely be circled in red as a hideous shortcoming in Western storytelling. In addition, this twist often alters the tone of the story so radically that it jumps genres.

Phrased another way, there is the idea in Western storytelling of a contract with the audience. The wisdom is that the audience will go along with a story, regardless of the preposterousness of its conventions, as long as the creators clearly and transparently signal to the audience at the beginning what kind of story they're signing up for and then never swerve out of that lane. Thus, you do not signal a gritty World War II drama that suddenly breaks into a synchronized song-and-dance number after the halfway point. You do not signal an uplifting story about an inspirational math teacher in a tough urban school that suddenly becomes dominated by a serial killer with a meat cleaver after the halfway point. Viewers would revolt. There would be TV remote–shaped holes in screens across America. Because you made a promise, and you reneged on it.

The four-act structure, on the other hand, is defined by a promise to swerve out of the expected lane.

Let's break down the story "Spring, Summer, Asteroid, Bird" into its four acts.

ACT ONE—The Introduction of the Main Elements

Chelsea versus Marilyn. They are distant cousins. They are also dinosaurs. Specifically, they are both theropods. Chelsea is an avian dinosaur, aka a bird. Marilyn is a tyrannosaur.

ACT TWO—The Development of the Main Elements

Chelsea lays eggs. Marilyn couldn't care less.

ACT THREE—The Twist/New Element

Asteroid! Note how the story pivots from a cozy, if weird, pastoral about two cousins who dislike each other to something cosmic and apocalyptic in scale. It stops being an Attenborough day-in-the-wild life story featuring two animals and becomes a story about astronomy and extinction—one that involves every living thing on the planet. The twist is intensified here by the switch in point of view and tense from third-person past tense to first-person present tense.

ACT FOUR—The Harmonizing of All Elements

The asteroid has wiped out most food except seeds. Chelsea is a bird, so she has a small mouth and a beak. Small mouth + beak = good for finding and eating seeds. Marilyn is large and has teeth, which equals bad for eating seeds. Chelsea prevails. The asteroid has revealed a new aspect of Chelsea's and Marilyn's relationship. Being small, having a beak, and eating seeds end up as massive advantages that neither cousin could have predicted. Notions of advantage and disadvantage have been turned upside down. Extinction-level events always create winners and losers, but the unexpected nature of the new element has revealed invisible strengths and weaknesses.

"THE DAUGHTERS OF ITOYA"

Rai San'yō was a historian, scholar, and poet who lived in Japan during the Edo period, in the late eighteenth and early nineteenth centuries. He composed a four-line poem called "The Daughters of Itoya" that serves as an elegant demonstration of the four-act structure at work:

The daughters of Itoya, Honmachi, Osaka.

One sister is sixteen, one sister is fourteen.

Daimyo of various regions kill with bows and arrows.

Itoya's daughters kill with their eyes.

Now, that's a weird story, but let's savor what it's doing.

ACT ONE—The Introduction of the Main Elements
The first act introduces the two daughters and the setting.

ACT TWO—The Development of the Main Elements
The second act just seems to develop those same elements. We don't have much information about the daughters, but we can make some assumptions about their relationship: close enough in age for them to have perhaps grown up playing together, but far enough apart for

there to be an older/younger sister dynamic. Thus, the entire first half seems to be a quiet, domestic story about life in historic Japan.

ACT THREE—The Twist/New Element

The third act injects a seemingly random element of war and violence with the introduction of the daimyo—powerful Japanese lords under whom warriors and soldiers served. This new element comes as a surprise and has no apparent relationship with the elements that came before (two daughters, domestic setting). Note how the twist appears to change the very genre of the story from a family story into a story of war. Further, the location of the new element so late in the story creates a more powerful sense of surprise. The unforeseen appearance of this element here creates a sense of invasion in our story that captures the sisters' own shock at having war enter their quiet life in a way that would have been impossible if the war element had been foreshadowed.

ACT FOUR—The Harmonizing of All Elements

The fourth act shows that the elements in the first two acts, the daughters, actually do have a relationship with the new third-act element, the warriors, in that the daughters are able to defeat them. The fourth act harmonizes the preceding elements by showing the relationship among the elements in a way that itself feels like a new element (possibly a supernatural one). Adding such a new element or new revelations about the preceding elements so late in a story would be met with disapproval in Western storytelling. However, the late introduction of war here followed by the suddenness of the ending causes the story and ideas to linger. The story abruptly stops without answering all the questions it suggests, which causes the reader to continue thinking about it afterward. Do the daughters literally kill with their eyes? Are they sorceresses? Was this metaphorical, like some sexist stereotype of girls seducing soldiers with their eyes only to murder them in their sleep? Or some satire of such a sexist stereotype? We don't know. We'll never know. As a result, we are left participating in the story by perpetuating it beyond the end of the page, and by writing potential explanations for its ending. The story lives on in a way that wouldn't be possible with a less abrupt, more fully unpacked ending.

How would this story act if it were a typical, well-behaved Western story? Picture a hipster coffee house in Silverlake, California. Every coffee drinker sits with a laptop, every laptop displays the screenplay they are working on. One of the screenwriters is working on something called *Daughters of Steel and Fire* (alternate title *Sisters of Blood and Ash*). Here's the three-act breakdown.

ACT ONE—Setup

Two daughters in historic Japan hide their secret powers from their strict father. One of them loves books and is able to use her eyes to read anything, even minds. The other loves martial arts and has the ability to see where an enemy's weapon will be in five seconds. They secretly train to defend their home against an ancient Evil that is prophesied to return. Their father fears strong female protagonists because reading books and doing martial arts were what killed their mother. He tries to force the girls into arranged marriages.

ACT TWO—Confrontation

The sisters flee the arranged marriages and disappear into the mountains. There, they find a secret temple of warrior nuns who help them hone their abilities into devastating weapons. The ancient Evil that threatens to destroy their world is amassing its army of resurrected soldiers. Due to shocking second-act betrayals and plot reversals, the sisters find themselves the last hope of humanity to defeat the forces of darkness.

ACT THREE—Resolution

The sisters ride into battle against the ancient Evil. One sister uses her power to read the minds of the soldiers and predict their movements. The other uses her power to see what blows the soldiers are about to execute before they do so. The sisters hack through the army culminating in a battle with the Dark One himself. They discover, to their shock, that the ancient foe is . . . their father! In his villain's infodump, he explains how he murdered their mother because she threatened to become a strong female protagonist. They battle him desperately, showing him their strength and independence. He is left hanging by his claw-like fingernails at the edge of the cliff. The girls attempt to save him but his own petty attempts to assert patriarchy cause him to plummet to his death, getting the girls to the right story ending but leaving their hands clean. The girls grieve the loss of their father but stand proud, for they have owned their power and found themselves.

Still awake?

This version forefronts tension, conflict, and resolution. Conflict is central now, between the sisters and their father, the sisters and the ancient Evil, their father and their mother.

Symmetry is satisfied because the element of the war against the great Evil is introduced in the first act and resolved by the final act. So is the supernatural element of the sisters' special eye powers. There is no late-in-the-game genre bait-and-switch. The genre remains constant throughout: historical fantasy with a cosmetic Japanese exterior that fails to cover an Americanized interior.

PARASITE

On first introduction, the four-act structure might strike you as alien or unsatisfying. However, you likely have already experienced examples of this story form without realizing it. Bong Joon-Ho's film *Parasite* is a superb example of the four-act structure. In case it didn't fly onto your radar, *Parasite* is a dazzling South Korean film about class struggle that swept the Oscars and became the first foreign-language film to win Best Picture. If you haven't seen the film, I am going to issue the sternest possible warning to watch it first and return to this section afterward. I would mourn spoiling the plot of *Parasite* for you as I would be depriving you of one of the great pleasures of early twenty-first-century cinema.

Given the intricacy of *Parasite*'s plot, it is useful to first conduct a full-body scan of the story's structure in order to reveal an overview of its four-act bones.

ACT ONE—The Introduction of the Main Elements

A poor family struggles to make ends meet. The son and daughter infiltrate a rich family and secure jobs with them through clever con games.

ACT TWO—The Development of the Main Elements

The poor family escalates the con games to oust innocent employees in the household and replace them with the family's father and mother.

ACT THREE—The Twist/New Element

The poor family discovers that there is someone even poorer living below them, socially and literally—the husband of the ousted former housekeeper.

ACT FOUR—The Harmonizing of All Elements

The rich, poor, and even poorer families wreak revenge on the people they blame for their plight.

Now, let's unpack the story in more detail and analyze how each section is achieving the classic purposes of the four-act structure.

ACT ONE—The Introduction of the Elements

Meet the Kims. They are a family of four in South Korea trying to claw their way out of the poverty pit they are quicksanding into. The desperation of their lives would be comic if it did not so evidently strip them of their dignity.

The opportunity to bring some money into the household lands in front of the son, Ki-Woo. He secures an interview for a cushy job tutoring the daughter of a rich family. Ki-Woo's confident sister Ki-Jung deploys her Photoshop skills to fake university documents so Ki-Woo will look qualified in ways he cannot afford to be.

Ki-Woo goes to the rich family's spacious, airy, sprawling house where he is interviewed by the pupil's mother, Mrs. Park. Ki-Woo asks to meet for a session with the daughter, during which he makes a gutsy move and grabs her wrist, calls out her racing pulse, and exhorts her to attack her studies with confidence. Mrs. Park is impressed by his boldness and hires him instantly.

Before Ki-Woo leaves, Mrs. Park shows him the artwork of her nine-year-old son, whose sloppy crayon doodles she compares to Basquiat. She blames his unruliness on his artistic genius. Ki-Woo and his sister Ki-Jung conspire to have Ki-Jung pretend to be a sought-after art tutor and meet Mrs. Park. Ki-Jung requests to have a trial session with the son. Mrs. Park asks to sit in on the session, but Ki-Jung confidently banishes her from the room.

When they finish their session, the son is completely tamed. Ki-Jung explains that a recurring scribble in the lower-right region of many of his paintings is a manifestation of psychosis and evidence of schizophrenia. Mrs. Park is overwhelmed with concern, but she is also grateful that her stricken son will be under Ki-Jung's care. Ki-Jung explains that because what they will be doing is not simple tutoring but art therapy, it will be charged at a very high rate. Mrs. Park gratefully agrees.

In the first act, we think we know what kind of story we are watching. This is a dark comedy/social satire. Ki-Woo and Ki-Jung charm us with their confidence. Mrs. Park in fact rewards both Ki-Woo and Ki-Jung with offers of employment because they are not obsequious and they act with boldness. Ki-Woo disarms Mrs. Park and his prospective student with his bravado. Ki-Jung cobbles together compelling credentials for the two of them with Photoshop, some Googling, ad-libbing, and nerve.

Mrs. Park comes across as easy to play. She and her husband seem pretty decent, if a little gullible. However, Ki-Woo's and Ki-Jung's scams don't seem to hurt the Parks any more than the loss of a mosquito belly's worth of blood would hurt a rhinoceros. So we know whom to root for, whom to mock (even with some amount of gentleness), what kind of story we are watching, and what the likely outcome will be (some sort of recognition of common humanity between the two classes).

ACT TWO—The Development of the Main Elements

Emboldened by their success, Ki-Woo and Ki-Jung help their parents infiltrate the Park household as well. They frame Mr. Park's young driver to look like he was engaging in illicit acts in the car and get him fired. They then manage to get their father, Mr. Kim, hired as the new driver.

The last position is for the mother, Mrs. Kim. The Parks already have an excellent housekeeper, Moon-Gwang, who was the housekeeper for the original architect/owner of the house, and thus has lived there the longest. They learn that Moon-Gwang is violently allergic to peach fuzz. Ki-Woo, Ki-Jung, and Mr. Kim embark on their greatest con of all. They execute an elaborate scheme involving peach fuzz, a secret selfie, and some hot sauce masquerading as blood to convince Mrs. Park that Moon-Gwang has tuberculosis and is lying about it. Moon-Gwang is fired and flushed out of the house immediately.

Mrs. Kim soon claims the position of housekeeper in the Park household.

The Parks' young son points out that all of the Kims smell the same, although of course the Parks have no idea that the Kims are actually all members of the same family and live in one household.

The second act utilizes the same elements as the first act and develops them further. Thus, we see the same families, the Kims and the Parks. The same dynamic of installing Kim family parasites onto the Park family's oblivious body drives this act, as in act one.

However, this time the cons are escalated. The cons in this act are cleverer, require more planting of evidence, and require multiple steps to pull off. Framing Mr. Park's driver requires Ki-Jung to discreetly strip off her underwear while riding in the car with the driver. Framing Moon-Gwang requires tailing her to what seems like a doctor's appointment, along with the precisely timed deployment of peach fuzz and the carefully angled squirting of hot sauce onto a napkin plucked from the trash.

Further, the emotional costs are raised in these latest two cons. In the first act, the cons are seemingly victimless crimes. Ki-Woo and Ki-Jung are not ousting other employees; they are just creating positions for themselves in a wealthy household. In the second act, two innocent employees who seem to be doing excellent work are shoved out of the Park nest without regard for their fate. However, the film manages to distract viewers from tasting this slightly sour moral note by leveling up the complexity and fun of the cons and getting us invested in seeing whether the elaborate traps the Kims have constructed will operate as planned. Thus, the film maintains the tone and genre established by the first act.

ACT THREE—The Twist/New Element

Soon thereafter, the Parks go on a family camping trip. The Kims seize the opportunity to lounge about the house, get drunk, eat the Parks' food, and fantasize about what life might be like if this house were theirs. Mr. Kim claims that this is their home now, but Mrs. Kim scoffs, saying that if Mr. Park walked in right now, her husband would run and hide like a cockroach.

In the middle of their revelry, the doorbell rings. The security camera shows that it is the former housekeeper, Moon-Gwang. She explains that she left something important behind, but the Parks push her out so quickly that she has no opportunity to collect it. She begs Mrs. Kim as her replacement to allow her in. Mrs. Kim relents.

Moon-Gwang hurries into the basement. Mrs. Kim goes down to find Moon-Gwang opening a secret door into a dimly lit subterranean passage. Mrs. Kim follows her down to find a man living in squalid conditions beneath the basement. Moon-Gwang explains that her husband Geun-Sae has been living in this nuclear bomb shelter for over four years, in hiding from debtors who threatened his life. She offers to pay Mrs. Kim if Mrs. Kim will keep their secret. Mrs. Kim starts to call the police.

However, Moon-Gwang discovers the rest of Mrs. Kim's family eavesdropping. Moon-Gwang recognizes all of them and begins recording the scene. Ki-Woo slips up and refers to Mr. Kim as "Dad." Moon-Gwang threatens to send the video evidence to the Parks and turn in this family of charlatans.

Now it is the Kims' turn to beg for sympathy, and Moon-Gwang returns their earlier pitilessness in kind. However, the Kims catch Moon-Gwang off guard, disarm her of the phone, delete the video, and disable her and her husband.

In the middle of this, Mrs. Park calls, saying that the camping trip was cancelled, and the Parks will be home in eight minutes. The Kims scramble to stuff Moon-Gwang and Geun-Sae back in the nuclear shelter and clean up the mess from their revelry, and then everyone except Mrs. Kim hides under the living room table.

The Parks' son announces that he wants to pitch his tent in the yard and camp in the rain. His parents indulge him and decide to sleep on the living room couch to keep an eye on him. They are unaware that their driver, tutor, and art therapist are hiding under the table just feet away, and Mr. Park comments on the Kims' smell, which he likens to boiled rags, adding further sting to the ignominy of having to hide under the Parks' table like cockroaches, as Mrs. Kim predicted.

The three Kims finally sneak out, flee into the pouring rain, and return home to find that their basement apartment is entirely flooded and they are homeless.

What makes the four-act structure so different from Western story structures is the third-act twist that introduces a new element. Western stories would foreshadow the surprise element beginning in act one and would gradually ramp up to the twist. In the four-act structure, there is no gradual progression. Whatever clues to the third-act surprise that might be seeded in earlier for continuity purposes are subtle and don't announce themselves as foreshadowing. Instead, there is a steep spike, which heightens the emotional shock of the surprise.

This emotional shock is what makes *Parasite* so powerful. After two acts during which we root for the Kims as they lay their charming traps, our story hits the third act like a waiter roller-skating over a pothole with a tray of champagne flutes. Suddenly, the story is in free fall, and we are tumbling with it. We don't know whom to root for anymore. Our charming rogues are now oppressors of people even worse off than they are, and they don't respond to the plight of this other family with much grace or graciousness. Further, the third-act twist changes the very genre of the story, as we are catapulted out of a dark comedy/social satire that might take swipes at a particular social class but never draws blood. Now, in the third act, we are literally drawing blood, and the movie becomes . . . well, what does it become? A thriller? A horror movie? Whatever it becomes, the tonal shift is radical and undeniable, from the moment we enter the green-lit stairway descending into the nuclear shelter, a scene that is scored with horror-movie violin crescendos.

ACT FOUR—The Harmonizing of All Elements

The next morning, all the Kims are summoned back to the Park household for the son's birthday party. As the guests gather, Ki-Woo becomes curious about how Moon-Gwang and Geun-Sae are doing in the basement. He sneaks down and discovers Moon-Gwang, apparently dead. Geun-Sae brings a stone sculpture down on Ki-Woo's head, grievously injuring him.

Geun-Sae rushes into the birthday party with a knife and stabs Ki-Jung. The Parks' young son faints at the sight. Mrs. Kim stabs Geun-Sae with a barbecue skewer, and he falls on top of Mr. Park's car keys. Mr. Park reaches for the keys under Geun-Sae to drive his son to the hospital, ignoring Ki-Jung bleeding out. Mr. Park holds his nose at the smell of Geun-Sae. At the sight of this, Mr. Kim snaps. He grabs Geun-Sae's knife and stabs not Geun-Sae, the man who stabbed his daughter, but Mr. Park instead. In the chaos that ensues, Mr. Kim flees into the nuclear shelter basement.

Ki-Jung bleeds to death. Ki-Woo survives his injuries, but he and his mother are sentenced to probation.

The new owners of the house remain oblivious to the fact that Mr. Kim is living beneath them, living off their leftovers in a parasitic relationship. Ki-Woo dreams of the bright day when he will be able to buy that house and his father will rise from the basement into the light.

The fourth act brings all the elements together and shows that they have an intimate relationship with each other, even if that relationship wasn't obvious before. Rich family, poor family (acts one and two), and even poorer family (act three) are all bound to one another. The parasitic relationship runs in multiple directions, with the rich family that cannot feed or pick up after itself, the poor families feeding off the rich family, and the poor families pitted against each other. It seems like Mr. Kim comes to a revelation at the end. He sees Mr. Park reaching under Geun-Sae for his keys to drive his son to the hospital while ignoring the other dying people around him and wrinkling his nose at the smell of Geun-Sae. Mr. Kim never admitted that he was stung by the Parks' prior comments about the way the Kims smelled. Now, Mr. Kim's rage over that disdain ignites some sort of understanding and a moment of class affinity with the man who just stabbed his daughter. It is as if he views with clarity for an instant the fact that the system that keeps people like Mr. Park in power is the same system that pits poor people against each other instead of against the people who suppress them.

But the movie doesn't tie things up neatly. Mr. Kim shrinks in apology for his act, but why? Is it because he changes his mind about what seemed in a moment of crisis like a political revelation but was actually an act of senselessness, or because he recoils from using murder to express even justified rage? Is it regret for punishing a specific person for systemic injustices, especially a person who was overall benevolent to Mr. Kim? We don't know. We'll never know. Further, his son Ki-Woo's greatest dream, after all these tragedies, remains the same: join that societal structure and buy that house. Ki-Woo doesn't want to topple the system—he wants to be at the top of it. And I have had conversations with multiple people, all immigrants, who found the film enthralling but whose final sentiment was "Why were all the poor people so greedy and ungrateful?" These are only anecdotal responses. However, it would be interesting to use *Parasite* as a litmus test. Play it for audiences of all kinds: Western and Eastern, liberal and conservative, American-born and immigrant, young and old, poor and wealthy. I would not be surprised if many of the people who feel that *Parasite* resonates with them were to discover that it resonates with others for completely opposite reasons.

All these differing interpretations and conflicting responses to the ending of *Parasite* are typical features of act four of the four-act structure. It elucidates the hitherto invisible strings connecting all the elements in the prior acts and then ends abruptly, often without clear or easy resolution, so that the story continues to echo in our heads long after the movie ends.

As another way to appreciate how perfect a specimen of the four-act structure *Parasite* is, let's ask ourselves what a traditional three-act Hollywood version of *Parasite* might look like and examine how the two would differ. The first question to consider is what genre studio executives would slot *Parasite* into. Black comedy? Family drama? Social justice story? Thriller? Horror? The genre might affect how cheery or pessimistic the ending would be, but it probably wouldn't prevent the story from getting significantly tidier and simpler. My guess is that the film would most likely turn out as a very familiar social justice story about class struggle with elements of black comedy, and that it would have no room in it for the moral confusion created by the new third-act element. It would probably look something like this:

ACT ONE—Setup

Poor family embarks on con game against rich family.

ACT TWO—Confrontation

Con game climaxes in confrontation where truths are shared.

ACT THREE—Resolution

Two families come to understand that they have more in common with each other than they realized because *people are people.*

Whether the two families overcome their differences by the end credits would probably depend on whether the executives wanted to foreground the social justice aspect or the black comedy aspect (as well as test-audience feedback). Regardless, I think it is clear how radically different the themes and tone of this Westernized version of *Parasite* would be from those of the original.

NINTENDO (*MARIO* AND *ZELDA* GAMES)

The four-act structure isn't limited to traditionally narrative media. Video games are an interactive medium, and Nintendo's video games often employ the four-act structure delightfully. We know Nintendo to be a video game company that makes highly interactive digital toys; many who follow the games industry also think of Nintendo as one of the mightiest forces pushing digital entertainment forward. Nintendo led the vanguard in digital fitness (Wii Fit), 3D screens that didn't require glasses (Nintendo 3DS), and facial recognition as early as 2011 (again, the Nintendo 3DS). However, despite their innovation, Nintendo is actually quite an old company. In fact, as strange as it might sound, Nintendo was founded before the end of the Ottoman Empire. A quick analysis of Nintendo's video games reveals that the older code of kishōtenketsu is braided into their DNA.

This code is on display in Nintendo's iconic *Mario* games. For those of you unfamiliar with the series, *Mario* games feature a mustachioed plumber who jumps, leaps, and bounces around various virtual playgrounds. The main appeal of the games is using Mario's arsenal of acrobatic moves to navigate, interact with, and manipulate his environments in a sort of safe, candy-colored take on parkour. Let's unpack one level from *Super Mario Odyssey* (Nintendo Switch) that incorporates zippers.

ACT ONE—The Introduction of the Main Elements

You control Mario. You swim into a shallow pool. The left wall of the pool has a zippered seam. You utilize an ability to "possess" the zipper. You guide the zipper to unzip along its three-sided seam, causing a panel in the wall to fall open, revealing coins. You dispossess the zipper and swim to collect the coins.

Act one thus sets up the main elements: you as Mario; zippers as doors.

ACT TWO—The Development of the Main Elements

You swim farther to a temple at one end of the pool. You find another zipper there. You possess this zipper, unzip along the seam, and reveal an opening in the temple's floor. This leads to another pool, in which you find another zipper that opens a panel in a wall. You then find a fourth zipper. You unzip this to enter a whole other zipper world.

Act two develops the main elements: you as Mario; zippers as more doors.

ACT THREE—The Twist/New Element

There are several new elements in this third act. First, you aren't swimming, you're maneuvering on platforms over a bottomless drop-off. Second, this world is more abstract, geometric, and surreal than the pool and temple areas. Third, the zippers here are also transformed, in that you unzip them to make sections fall, thus forming bridges that allow you to cross chasms. Fourth, and most significantly, the area is now crawling with enemies that you have to avoid or eliminate by bouncing on them, which is perilous given how narrow the bridges are.

Act three changes the look and feel of the world, transforms the zippers into bridges, and adds in the unexpected element of enemies.

ACT FOUR—The Harmonizing of All Elements

At the far end of this zipper world is a flat plane. The key that you are questing for floats at the end of it. You need to cross the plane, but enemies meander about. You run to the key and grab it. However, your return is now blocked by the swarm of enemies that have migrated toward you. Racing back the way you came is impossible. Then you realize that this plane is in essence a wide bridge over a chasm, and there is a zipper down its middle. You don't have to defeat the legion of enemies. You simply possess the zipper and unzip the bridge that your enemies are standing on. The bridge falls open into two panels, sending your enemies tumbling down into the chasm below. You dispossess the zipper safely at the other end and go on your way.

This fourth act shows that the zippers introduced and developed in the first two acts and the new third-act elements (zippers as bridges, enemies) have a relationship. The zippers and their use as bridges can be used to defeat the enemies without fighting.

An even more ingenious example of a Nintendo game that utilizes the four-act structure is *The Legend of Zelda: A Link between Worlds* (Nintendo 3DS). For those of you unfamiliar with this series, the *Zelda* games are some of the most beloved and celebrated adventure games of all time. You play as an elfin boy named Link, who quests to help a princess named Zelda. Features of the series include vast, explorable worlds and ingenious puzzles masquerading as manipulable environments, such as mechanical temples and clockwork dungeons.

This particular entry in the series features a mechanism that empowers Link to press up against a wall and transform into a flat painting done in a cartoonish Chagall style. As a painting, he is powerless. He can neither attack nor defend himself. However, he can creep along walls, inching to the side and following the surface around corners. He utilizes this ability to reach otherwise inaccessible places, to enter rooms through windows protected by bars, and so on. This ability is used to brilliant effect in the game's final boss battle (an elaborate and more difficult fight against a unique enemy with powers and weaknesses that you have to figure out and exploit).

ACT ONE—The Introduction of the Main Elements

You are trapped in an octagonal tower with a monster named Yuga. The close quarters constitute a massive disadvantage to you, since you are kept within striking distance of Yuga almost all the time. Thus, as you scamper to dodge Yuga's formidable attacks, the tower wall itself is your enemy as much as Yuga is. The tight, enclosed quarters from which you cannot escape are a major obstacle and defining feature of this section.

Act one lays out the main elements: you as Link; Yuga; and a small, locked room.

ACT TWO—The Development of the Main Elements

Once you land several hits on Yuga, he employs new, even more difficult attacks. For example, Yuga begins a game of electric volleyball. He sends a ball of energy at you. If you hit it with a correctly timed sword strike, you will send the ball back at him. He will return the ball to you with a strike of his own. The volleys go back and forth, faster and faster. Miss the timing, and you get electrocuted. Eventually, Yuga will miss and be electrocuted. You rush in to take a slash at him and do damage.

Act two develops the same elements as in act one: you as Link; Yuga; and a small, locked room.

ACT THREE—The Twist/New Element

Then commences an ingenious three-tiered fight. Yuga becomes a 2D painting himself and retreats to the tower wall around you. He is invulnerable to your sword attacks as a painting, you cannot attack with your sword when you are a 2D painting yourself, and you have no way to force him off the wall into a vulnerable 3D figure again. The retreat of Yuga to the 2D state feels like a new third-act element on its own, but there is an even more blatant addition: the heroine Zelda descends from above to make you a heavenly gift, the Bow of Light. It's a weapon that can only be used when you are a 2D painting.

The Bow of Light represents an entirely new gameplay mechanic that is like nothing that has come before it. Before, all you could do as a 2D painting was inch along walls to access otherwise inaccessible areas or spy on events in rooms you couldn't reach. The Bow of Light changes that entirely by adding combat. However, the 2D wall combat comes with its own quirky mechanics. You learn that Yuga is invulnerable from the front while he is on the wall as a 2D painting, and he is always turning quickly to face left or right so he faces toward you. Thus, you have to alternate between popping on the wall in 2D to get him to face in one direction, popping off the wall into 3D to scoot behind him, and popping back on the wall to let loose an arrow at his back before he realizes you're behind him and turns toward you. Hitting him with the 2D arrow pops him off the wall into his vulnerable 3D form so that you can continue to land hits on him with your sword. The battle escalates through multiple tiers of this combat mechanic as you toggle between 2D and 3D and Yuga manifests new and more powerful attack patterns.

The introduction of the Bow of Light radically changes the feel of the game. In the preceding dozens of hours of gameplay, you have used your ability to pop onto the wall in 2D form to navigate, not to fight. The addition of combat to the 2D painting mechanic is a revelation. It's as if someone who has only roller-skated their whole life is suddenly able to add combat to it, thus creating roller derby. Further, toggling between 2D and 3D requires precise timing, as does evading Yuga's attacks in either mode. It thus creates a rhythm to this section that makes it feel like a dance—like adding dance to martial arts and coming up with capoeira.

ACT FOUR—The Harmonizing of All Elements

In his final incarnation, Yuga is invulnerable from the front. Further, he has learned from your trick of popping off the wall and scooting behind him. Now, as soon as you pop back onto the wall, he instantly faces whatever direction you're standing in, and there is no momentary delay in his reaction for you to take advantage of, as there was in act three. You seemingly have no way to force him off the wall because you have no way to get behind him to take a shot with your arrow. This is where all the elements that preceded come together and reveal their hidden relationship. You were locked in this small, octagonal tower, which is essentially a circular cell, with this enemy who had an arsenal of powerful attacks. All this time, the wall was your enemy, herding you closer to danger. Then, in a third-act twist, your enemy started using the wall to hide, so the wall became both your barrier and his bunker.

However, now, in the fourth act, you realize that the wall's shape itself is a hidden gift. Instead of popping onto the wall, turning toward Yuga, and shooting your arrow in futility at his invulnerable front side, you turn in the other direction. You fire off an arrow. While Yuga remains facing toward you, ready to fend off your frontal attacks, the arrow travels in the other direction along the circular shape of the wall until it arrives at Yuga and strikes him in his unprotected back! You have turned the wall from a disadvantage into an advantage. Yuga used the two-dimensionality of the wall as a place to hide, and you turned the geometry of that against him.

Yuga pops off the wall, you land a final hit, and you defeat him.

Act four thus very satisfyingly harmonizes the elements that came before: you as Link; Yuga; the small, locked room; and the Bow of Light. You must use not just the Bow of Light to defeat Yuga, but the very shape of the small, locked room. The answer was lying in plain view literally all around you, and the thing that you considered an obstacle is actually your greatest weapon. The way the game gently nudges you to figure this out yourself makes you feel like a genius and makes this final battle against Yuga one of the most joyous episodes in all of gaming, in my opinion.

Other *Zelda* games expand on this by stringing sequences of kishōtenketsu together. I won't linger on *Zelda* games more for fear of never stopping, which is a very real danger, but fans of the series might try replaying these sequences from *The Legend of Zelda: The Ocarina of Time* (Nintendo 64/Nintendo GameCube/Nintendo 3DS) with strings of kishōtenketsu sequences in mind:

- Dampé's Crypt: Act three twist = Hookshot, which allows you access to Forest Temple
- Forest Temple: Act three twist = Fairy Bow
- Spirit Temple as Child Link: Act three twist = Silver Gauntlets, which allow you to enter Spirit Temple as Adult Link
- Spirit Temple as Adult Link: Act three twist = Mirror Shield

The fact that the four-act structure is integrated into the *Mario* and *Zelda* games, which are the most popular Nintendo series, debunks complaints that the structure is too strange or unpalatable for Western audiences. Tens of millions of children in Western countries have been enjoying kishōtenketsu their whole lives.

HARD-BOILED WONDERLAND AND THE END OF THE WORLD

"The Daughters of Itoya," *Parasite*, and the passages from *Mario* and *Zelda* games are classic examples of the four-act structure that introduce a clear new element in the third act. However, the introduction of a new element can manifest in more subtle ways, including as a radical reshuffling of the relationship among the preceding elements. Haruki Murakami's 1985 novel *Hard-Boiled Wonderland and the End of the World* presents an example of this. Murakami's books are marketed in the West as literary fiction, but they often swerve into other genre lanes, including Surrealism, science fiction, and fantasy. This book is a mashup of two plotlines in different genres. The first is a hard-boiled, near-future noir. The second is Surrealist fable. The organization of the two strands is quite simple. The hard-boiled plotline lives in the odd-numbered chapters. The Surrealist "end of the world" story lives in the even-numbered ones.

ACT ONE—The Introduction of the Main Elements

Hard-Boiled Wonderland (HBW)

The book begins with the narrator in near-future Tokyo accepting a job for a quasi-governmental entity working as something called a Calcutec, a sort of human encryptor of data. He is led into a lab hidden deep under Tokyo by the Girl, a capable, cheerful young woman. The Girl's grandfather, the Professor, runs the lab, which employs

Calcutecs to launder data by shuffling it through the hemispheres of their brains. The Professor isolates a sector of the narrator's consciousness behind a sort of firewall.

End of the World (EOW)

The protagonist, who might or might not be connected to the narrator in the HBW sections, finds himself in a Town of emotionless, perhaps mindless, people, enclosed by a Wall. The Town is filled with beasts resembling unicorns. Upon arrival, the Gatekeeper amputates and imprisons the protagonist's Shadow. The protagonist meets with the Librarian, who helps him do his work as the Dreamreader to "liberate" dreams from the Library's collection of unicorn skulls.

Act one establishes that there are two storylines in this book, each happening in a different world and presented in alternating chapters. The first world is gritty and contemporary and has a faint aroma of cyberpunk. The second world is dreamy and feels like it's composed of Jungian archetypes. Act one of the book sets out the main elements in each world—a principal male character, whose job is to process particular information, enters an unfamiliar environment and meets with a kindly female guide as well as a strange authority figure who partitions off an element of the main character's mind or self. Despite the difference in the tones of the two worlds, the storylines inhabiting them clearly rhyme with each other.

ACT TWO—The Development of the Main Elements

Hard-Boiled Wonderland

The Professor gives the narrator an unusual animal skull. The narrator consults a Librarian, who might or might not be related to the Librarian in the EOW section, for help in identifying the skull. Like the Girl, this Librarian is cheerful, capable, and pretty, and she has a magnificent appetite for food. Then, dastardly events begin to cascade onto the narrator: he finds himself sucked into a factional war over control of the shuffling of data between the government, which backs the Calcutecs, and the defectors, who seek to pirate or "liberate" the data from the governmental monopoly.

End of the World

When autumn arrives, the Dreamreader is finally permitted to visit his severed and imprisoned Shadow. His Shadow asks him to study the Town and create a map of it. Working on the map makes the Dreamreader grow ill. At last, he is able to deliver the map to his Shadow, who is now also very sick but hopes to use the map to escape from the Town.

Act two sees the main characters in both sections become more embroiled in the mysterious worlds they have entered. In the HBW sections, the main character is entangled in factional fighting in this strange information laundering field in which he finds himself. In the EOW section, the main character is learning from the severed part of his self about the strange Town in which he finds himself.

ACT THREE—The Twist/New Element

Hard-Boiled Wonderland

The Girl convinces the narrator to return to her grandfather's lab underneath Tokyo. They find the lab destroyed, probably by the Calcutec defectors/pirates. The Professor explains that the Town, and the entire world in the EOW chapters, is the sector of the narrator's consciousness that the Professor isolated behind a firewall in the initial procedure. Further, the procedure will cause the narrator's brain to shut down in twenty-four hours, and the Professor cannot reverse that due to the destruction of his lab.

However, even though the narrator's body will power down shortly, he and the Town in his mind can live what appears subjectively to him to be an infinite amount of time. The Professor likens the process to encoding an encyclopedia on a toothpick, which is a thought experiment that uses math to question the idea of eternity.

End of the World

With the help of the Librarian, the Dreamreader finds stacks of unicorn skulls, which they learn are vessels for the townspeople's souls. The Dreamreader then visits his dying Shadow. The Shadow wants the two of them to use the map to escape and be rejoined as one. However, the Dreamreader balks, having grown fond of the circumscribed life in the Town. The Shadow explains to the Dreamreader that the townspeople have all had their minds removed. The unicorn beasts soak up the remnants of the people's minds. The Dreamreader's job is to "read" the skulls to dissipate the last traces of the townspeople's minds in them. The cost of continuing to live in the paradise of the Town is the loss of the mind.

The book offers a less classic and more exotic "new element" in the third act. The two braided worlds are united in the first two acts by thematic rhymes and undeniable echoes. These operate like foreshadowing to suggest some forthcoming revelation about the relationship between the two worlds. However, when it does come, the truth is so structurally disruptive that it feels like an entirely new element.

To appreciate how act three of the book is achieving this, we need to sketch out the encyclopedia/toothpick thought experiment in more detail. Suppose you assign a number after a decimal point to each letter in the alphabet. For example, if the letter "a" were assigned the number one, the letter "b" were assigned the number two, and the letter "c" were assigned the number three, you could encode the word "cab" by making a single mark at the point on the toothpick that represents .312 (or 31.2 percent) of its total length. The entire contents of the encyclopedia could theoretically be converted with this method, resulting in a decimal point with many, many numbers following it. If you could make a mark with sufficient accuracy, you could capture the entire text of the encyclopedia with one mark, which someone with the code could read. Even if it would require subatomic precision to locate and mark that point, it is still conceivably possible.

The Professor in the HBW world uses this thought experiment to break it to the main character that the EOW sections are happening inside the narrator's brain, partitioned behind a neurological firewall. Thus, this work of fiction reveals that half its substance is fiction within fiction. The third act has one half of the book swallowing the other. Or is it spawning or disgorging the other half? Either way, it slaps us with a radical reshuffling of our understanding of the relationship among the preceding elements.

The revelation about unseen relationships among prior elements usually happens in the fourth act. However, when it occurs in the third act of this book, it's such a trippy revelation, almost a Philip K. Dick or M. Night Shyamalan plot twist, that it truly feels like a wholly new element. In terms of genre, the third-act twist also pivots the book out of noir cyberpunk and Surrealist fable into a more philosophical or classically literary fiction examination of what eternity means.

It also sends the book into a more profound exploration of our personal experience of time. The encyclopedia thought experiment and the proposition that the narrator can live an infinite time in the Town in his mind within a finite time in the outer world train our attention on how we mark the passage of time in the first place. We measure it with machines and systems, but emotionally we mark it with details and events. We expect a certain regularity in the rhythm of details and events in our lives as we travel through time. However, we all know that details and events do not necessarily space themselves out regularly, and that the density or rate of their occurrence alters our perception of the passage of time. Dull, routine stretches in our lives unpunctuated by memorable markers can feel longer than they are or, for some people, can be condensed in memory into an accountably swift loss or waste of time. Momentous or emotional things, or events arriving in rapid succession, can make time seem to expand ("my whole life flashed before my eyes") or contract ("the time flew by"). This emotional relativity of time is a feature of everyone's lived experience and a reminder that our experience of time is largely subjective, not objective, and that our internal metrics for it are qualitative and personal, not quantitative and universal.

ACT FOUR—The Harmonizing of All Elements

Hard-Boiled Wonderland

The Girl and the narrator return to the surface of Tokyo. The narrator spends what might be his remaining mortal time eating, listening to music cassettes, watching the rain, and otherwise seeming to imbibe deeply in these last fleeting hours to experience eternity by experiencing individual moments in as much detail as he can.

End of the World

The Dreamreader learns that his Shadow was able to study the map and discern a way to escape the Town. However, the Dreamreader ultimately declines to leave with his Shadow. The Dreamreader can't depart because he understands on some level that he created everything in this Town. He chooses to live there in the tiny infinity of that sheltered space.

The final act of the book explores the idea that eternity and immortality are not about the breadth of time we live but about the detail in which we experience each instant, and the depth at which we inhabit even a moment. Thus, the narrator in the HBW world spends what might be his last hours of life absorbing details: the rough voice of Bob Dylan on the stereo, the flight of birds.

I find this idea beautiful because its natural extrapolation is that sensitive people experience more time and live more life because they absorb more of the details and events populating the time they pass through. People with sensitive natures often have to wrestle with challenges other people might not—for instance, impostor syndrome, self-doubt, pessimism, and so on. The idea that the upside to all of that is that sensitive people don't just live more fully, but are, in a sense, getting more time on this planet and experiencing more life, is quietly powerful.

YOUR NAME

This bittersweet animated fantasy/romance directed by Makoto Shinkai was an international sensation. It was the third-highest-grossing Japanese film of all time and received numerous international awards. It generated much online discussion about whether Makoto Shinkai was the heir to the throne of master animated filmmaker Hayao Miyazaki.

ACT ONE—The Introduction of the Main Elements

The film begins with shots of a young woman and a young man. Voiceover statements refer to them looking for something ever since the comet.

Mitsuha is a high school student in a small town around a lake. The town is pastoral, quaint, and idyllic, but she chafes against small-town life. She dislikes being scrutinized for being the mayor's daughter. She wishes that she were a handsome boy in Tokyo. One day, she wakes up, but it is not actually Mitsuha, it is a boy inhabiting her body. He is unfamiliar with Mitsuha's life and with "wearing" a female body, with comic results. The next day, Mitsuha is restored to her body with no memory of the lost day. However, her notebook contains cryptic messages asking, "Who are you?"

Mitsuha wakes up one morning in the body of Taki, a high school boy in Tokyo. She is disoriented, unfamiliar with Taki's life and with inhabiting a male body, again with comic results. She ventures out into Tokyo, which appears to her a shimmering wonder. She fumbles through school and work in Taki's body, doing her best to figure out his routines. She assumes that this is a dream. She makes an entry in his phone journal about her day as him and writes her name on Taki's hand.

Taki wakes up with no memory of what happened. He sees Mitsuha's name on his hand and the phone journal entry he doesn't remember writing.

Mitsuha wakes up in her own body. She finds written on her arm, "Mitsuha, who are you? What are you?" She has no memory of the prior day but finds entries in her notebook.

In this first act, the main elements are set forth: Mitsuha, a girl in a small town; Taki, a boy in Tokyo; their inexplicable body switching; and their first attempts to communicate with each other, despite never inhabiting the same space at the same time. The genre is a mashup of comedy and body-switching supernatural story. The tone is farcical and rompy with the feel of a rom-com.

ACT TWO—The Development of the Main Elements

Although their memories of their adventures in the other person's body fade quickly upon return to their own bodies, Mitsuha and Taki simultaneously realize that their experiences are not dreams and that they are switching places. They coordinate by leaving notes for each other on their phones to find when they return to their own bodies. They lay down ground rules for behavior while in each other's bodies, and they decide to leave notes about what they did in each other's lives so they can act with continuity.

During one episode when Taki is inhabiting Mitsuha's body, Mitsuha's grandmother takes "her" and her little sister to visit a shrine relic in a mountaintop crater. The grandmother tells them that the local traditions of cord-braiding and wrapping ropes around trees represent the flow of time, and that time can be tangled, twisted, and undone. They view the achingly beautiful landscape and scan the sky for a comet that news reports say will soon pass near to the Earth. The grandmother says, "Oh, Mitsuha. You're dreaming right now, aren't you?"

Taki wakes up in his own body, weeping, although he can't remember why. He rushes to a date that Mitsuha made on his behalf with Miss Okudera, a pretty coworker that Mitsuha has been flirting with while in Taki's body. During the date, they visit a photo exhibition and Taki sees a landscape that he recognizes from when he inhabited Mitsuha's body. The date ends with Miss Okudera's noting that Taki seems distant, and like a different person.

Mitsuha imagines their date, with a bittersweet mix of emotions. Mitsuha left Taki a note saying that by the end of the date, it should be dark enough that Taki and Miss Okudera will be able to see the comet. Taki has no idea what she is talking about. Mitsuha views the comet in the night sky and sees a piece of it break off.

Act two develops the same elements set forth in act one: Mitsuha, Taki, their body switching, and their attempts to communicate. Their interactions through the notes they leave for each other on their phones become more elaborate, culminating with Mitsuha's using her time in Taki's body to flirt and set up a date with Miss Okudera. The interaction between Taki and Mitsuha becomes more emotionally complicated, too, as revealed in Taki's inability to be fully present during the date with someone else and Mitsuha's mix of emotions imagining the date. The rom-com tone is shifting from com to rom.

ACT THREE—The Twist/New Element

Taki tries to call the number that he thinks is Mitsuha's but receives a "no service" message. The body-switching episodes mysteriously stop. Without them, Mitsuha and Taki have no way to communicate with each other.

Taki draws views of Mitsuha's town from memory and tries to

research possible places it could be. Taki journeys out to the country in search of the town. While in a restaurant, a cook sees a picture Taki drew and recognizes the town as Itomori, which was blasted out of existence three years ago by a comet strike. Taki checks his phone. The journal entries that Mitsuha wrote to him while in his body disappear.

Taki researches the Itomori disaster and finds Mitsuha's name among the list of people killed. He realizes that he and Mitsuha aren't separated by just geographical distance; they are separated in time. They have not just been traveling across space to switch bodies; they have been traveling through time. Taki's world in Tokyo is taking place in the present. Mitsuha's story in the village took place three years earlier, shortly before the comet strike. Taki begins to wonder whether Mitsuha was just a dream built on a subconscious memory of a news report of the disaster, or else a ghost. With all evidence of the interaction gone, he begins to forget even her name.

The braided-cord bracelet that Taki wears triggers in him a faint memory of Mitsuha's grandmother explaining that time is a cord that connects different things. Inspired by this, Taki visits the remains of Itomori and finds the shrine in the middle of the mountaintop crater that Mitsuha's grandmother took them to. Inside the shrine, he finds the sake made at a village festival three years before from Mitsuha's own saliva. He takes a sip of the sake and is transported into a vision of Mitsuha's entire life up to the point when the comet strikes.

Three Years Before: Taki wakes up in Mitsuha's body. Mitsuha's grandmother recognizes that this is not Mitsuha. She reveals that both she and Mitsuha's mother also experienced similar things when they were younger, though the memories are greatly faded. Taki warns her that the comet is going to destroy Itomori.

Taki as Mitsuha tries to convince Mitsuha's father, the mayor, to evacuate the town, but he refuses. Taki's forceful nature makes the mayor realize that this is not his daughter. Mitsuha's sister mentions that Mitsuha spontaneously went to Tokyo the day before. Taki wonders if the real Mitsuha could be at the shrine relic at that moment in Taki's body. He visits the site.

Present: Mitsuha wakes up in Taki's body, three years after the comet strike, with no memory of how she got there. She looks down on the town and sees it has been obliterated. She asks herself if this means that she died. Mitsuha recalls being back in her own body the day before, which was really three years ago, and getting on the train to Tokyo to find Taki. She called the number she thought was his but also got a "no service" message. She saw him on a train and greeted him, but he didn't know her, because this was three years in his past, before the body-switching started.

Three Years Before: Taki in Mitsuha's body now remembers the incident from what is for him three years ago, when the strange girl he had never met before greeted him on the train. He runs to the rim of the rising hill surrounding the shrine.

Present: Mitsuha in Taki's body senses Taki's presence and runs around the rim of the hill surrounding the shrine, searching for him.

Three Years Before/Present: As they pass each other, they can sense each other's presence. At the moment of twilight, which they call "magic hour," they are able to see each other in their own bodies. She notices the corded-braid friendship bracelet he wears, and he returns it to her. She ties it in her hair. They decide to write down their names on each other's hands so they won't forget, as they have been doing after returning to their own bodies, but Mitsuha doesn't finish writing her name when magic hour ends and the connection is broken.

Present: Taki struggles to hold onto Mitsuha's name and why he came to the hill, but the memories slip away once again.

Three Years Before: Mitsuha, back in her own body and retaining memories of what Taki showed her, continues with her efforts to save the town. She and her friends hijack the town's public service announcement speaker system to broadcast a warning to evacuate. However, town authorities apprehend Mitsuha's friends and issue a reverse-order for the townsfolk to stay put. In the midst of the pandemonium, Mitsuha begins to forget Taki's name. She glances down where he wrote his name on her hand but the words there are "I love you." Meanwhile in Tokyo, Taki watches the comet pass overhead, unaware that it is headed to destroy the girl he will meet in three years. The comet strikes, obliterating Itomori, in a scene of terrible beauty.

Act three injects a new element into the story: time travel. It complicates the ability of Mitsuha and Taki to connect because they are not just separated by space, they are separated by time. Further, the revelation that they are separated in time leads to a further, more devastating revelation that Mitsuha might in fact already be dead in Taki's timeframe. The new time-travel element introduced lands like an asteroid in the overall story and in Mitsuha's and Taki's budding love story. It both explains what has come before and greatly complicates it. The new element of time travel is revealed to be both the mechanism by which the lovers came together and also the reason they might be separated forever. Thus, the third-act element presents a complicated "villain" for the story.

The act three twist also jumps the story from two genres into two other genres. The first two acts are a combination of comedy and body-switching supernatural story. The third-act twist turns the film into both a disaster movie and a time-travel story. The tone also shifts from farcical to urgent, wistful, and bittersweet.

Further, the love story pivots from rompy rom-com in the first two acts to something much more desperate and tragic, but also genuinely more romantic, with the third-act twist. Whatever romantic element had begun to emerge in the first two acts is transformed by the realization that the two of them might be irrevocably divided because one of them might very well already be dead. The romance stops focusing on a wacky and extreme meet cute and takes a hard turn into a story about star-crossed lovers whose fates seem ruled by cosmic events.

Finally, the twist accentuates the storytelling device of having Mitsuha and Taki communicate only by leaving messages for each other in their phone journals or writing words on their arms. The constricted mediums through which they communicate suddenly feel like the slenderest thread, a thread by which one of them is dangling over a chasm. This sense of urgency would be lost if they were able to talk freely and in real-time and to hear each other's voices instead of just reading each other's words. The pressure created by the limited mediums of communication creates heightened emotion and casts one of the elements introduced in act one in a far more desperate light.

Note that act three, in this case, begins somewhat before the midpoint of the film. The acts in the four-act structure are not necessarily uniform in length, just like the acts in the Western three-act structure. The acts are defined more by focus and function than run time or page count.

ACT FOUR—The Harmonizing of All Elements

Present: Taki awakes beside the remains of the town destroyed three years ago, with no memory of why he is there. He continues with his life in Tokyo, nursing an unnamable sense of trying to recover something or someone he has lost. Five years pass. Taki remains inexplicably obsessed with the comet strike and learns that most of the people survived because the town happened to be conducting a drill and evacuated the people to high ground just before the comet's impact. Looking at pictures of the lost town makes his chest feel tight. He constantly thinks he glimpses women in crowds with braided-cord hair bands that stir some recognition in him.

One day, he glimpses a stranger on a passing train and she glimpses him. They instantly recognize each other. They disembark their trains and try to find each other, but they grow shy when they do, and they pass each other on a set of stairs in silence. When Taki is unable to contain himself any longer, he turns and asks if he knows her. They are both overcome with inexplicable emotion. They ask simultaneously, "Could I ask you your name?"

Act four harmonizes all the elements that came before: Mitsuha, Taki, their body swapping, and the new time-travel element all have a relationship with each other. The third-act time-travel element explains the relationship among the elements that came before but also threatens to divide them from each other.

The fourth act reveals how all the elements relate to each other in a simple way: nothing stands in the way of true love and destiny. Time, physics, and catastrophic cosmic events cannot keep apart two people who are destined for each other. The third act "villain" cannot vanquish our hero and heroine. Love wins. The old-fashioned, unabashed romanticism of this fourth-act harmonizing serves as an unexpected and warm anchor for such an intricately plotted story. I think that it is this very romanticism that accounts for the film's popularity.

FOUR-ACT STRUCTURE IN WESTERN STORIES

The case studies I've shared have featured East Asian settings, characters, and/or creators. However, the four-act structure is absolutely not limited to East Asian settings, characters, and creators.

For example, I wrote a novelette entitled *The Ladies' Aquatic Gardening Society*, published in *Asimov's Science Fiction* magazine, that is set in Newport, Rhode Island, during the Gilded Age, and features a cast of all-White main characters. I won't include a detailed synopsis here, as you can read or listen to the novelette for free on my website, but here is a one-sentence summary:

Two grandes dames of the Gilded Age battle for position in Newport society by planting increasingly outrageous and environmentally devastating theme gardens.

And here is the structure breakdown:

ACT ONE—The Introduction of the Main Elements

Wealthy Newport society in the Gilded Age is ruled over by Mrs. Alva Vanderbilt. Mrs. Howland-Thorpe had been the favorite of Mrs. Vanderbilt until Mrs. Fleming, a worldly and overeducated Italian of noble lineage, came along. Mrs. Fleming becomes the favorite new pet of Mrs. Vanderbilt and is soon the center of attention in all of Newport society.

ACT TWO—The Development of the Main Elements

Until Mrs. Fleming arrived, Mrs. Howland-Thorpe's talent for planting novel and visually striking gardens had secured her elevated social status. In an effort to claw her new rival out of her seat as Mrs. Vanderbilt's pet, Mrs. Howland-Thorpe engages in a campaign to impress Newport society by building increasingly outrageous gardens around lavish themes. However, Mrs. Fleming plants an understated garden of her own, inspired by her Italian lineage, which wins the admiration of all. Meanwhile, Mrs. Howland-Thorpe's gardens are scorned for their tackiness. When Mrs. Howland-Thorpe tries to wreak revenge on Mrs. Fleming's garden by releasing burrowing moles and voles into it, the scheme backfires, causing the vermin to destroy her own garden as well as the gardens of their neighbors.

ACT THREE—The Twist/New Element

A new breed of rose is created by biologists. It looks like a rose but is able to grow in the sea. When the rights to the Sea-Rose are offered at auction, Mrs. Howland-Thorpe realizes that this novelty is her last chance to save her position in Newport Society. She spends exorbitantly to win the rights at auction. Mrs. Fleming begs Mrs. Howland-Thorpe not to plant the Sea-Rose, for it will destroy the ecology of the oceans around Newport. Mrs. Howland-Thorpe tells Mrs. Fleming to proverbially eat cake.

ACT FOUR—The Harmonizing of All Elements

Mrs. Howland-Thorpe builds an underwater theme garden with Sea-Roses that includes topiaries pruned in the shape of castles and landscapes that can be toured in a diving bell on tracks. At the debut of this aquatic marvel, Mrs. Fleming destroys the garden with explosives, much to Mrs. Howland-Thorpe's humiliation. However, in the aftermath, Mrs. Howland-Thorpe discovers some unusual strains of the Sea-Rose that were able to tolerate the blast. As she restores her crop from these hardy mutants, she discovers that they have other extraordinary qualities, such as the ability to root and blossom anywhere, even in the living flesh of whales, and to overwhelm all native plants. Mrs. Howland-Thorpe embarks on a grand mission to restore her reputation by planting the Sea-Rose in all the waters of the Earth.

The story is structured in classic kishōtenketsu. In act one, we are introduced to the main elements: Mrs. Howland-Thorpe, Mrs. Fleming, their rivalry, their Newport social circle, and the tradition of planting gardens to gain social status. It's a story of rich people behaving badly. Act two develops those same elements by making the gardens and the rivalry more outrageous. In this act, we see more extreme examples of humans devastating the natural world because they are entitled and self-absorbed. Act three drops the fictitious Sea-Rose into the rivalry. Act four shows how the Sea-Rose changes the rivalry, which ends up changing the ecology of the entire planet. Act four reveals the self-absorption of the humans introduced in the first two acts to be not mere pettiness on a personal scale, but something that will have apocalyptic global consequences.

This story also demonstrates how kishōtenketsu can be particularly appropriate for stories about unforeseen environmental consequences. Each main character's decision logically leads to the next decision and each effect logically flows from each decision, until the series of steps has somehow led the world to a bewilderingly unreasonable state. It creates the impression of a cascade of dominos that you didn't even realize were being set in place until they were already falling.

In terms of genre, for the first two acts, the story is a historical period piece and black comedy told in a dry mock-Austen style. The third-act twist changes the genre of the story into science fiction, specifically an environmental catastrophe story. The fourth act reveals the relationship among all the elements, showing how the third-act new element allowed the toxicity between the two main characters to spill into and alter the whole world.

Thus, *The Ladies' Aquatic Gardening Society* demonstrates that kishōtenketsu need not be limited only to stories with East Asian settings or characters.

Another example is Roald Dahl's *Matilda*. Act one introduces us to a precocious and brilliant girl named Matilda; her oblivious and neglectful parents; the tyrannical headmistress at her school, Miss Trunchbull; and her kind teacher, Miss Honey. Act two develops the same elements, and Matilda and her classmates play pranks on the unkind adults in their lives. Act three introduces a new element: Matilda can move objects with her mind! She also learns that Miss Honey is Miss Trunchbull's niece, and that Miss Trunchbull stole Miss Honey's house and her wages. Act four brings all these elements together: Matilda uses her telekinesis to move chalk with no visible hand and writes a note to Miss Trunchbull demanding she give back what belongs to Miss Honey. The book ends with Miss Trunchbull and Matilda's parents leaving, Matilda getting to live with Miss Honey, and Matilda's telekinetic powers disappearing now that she has proper stimulation for her mind.

The act three introduction of telekinesis makes the book jump genres. It starts out with the very familiar trope of brilliant child versus oppressive adults. While many elements are broad and cartoonish, there is nothing in the early part of the book that defies the laws of physics. Then the telekinesis comes out of seemingly nowhere to make the book leap the tracks over onto the paranormal rails. The paranormal element ends up resolving all the relationships among the elements that came before.

One of the best examples of the four-act structure in a Western setting is J. K. Rowling's *Harry Potter and the Prisoner of Azkaban*, the third book in a seven-part series. For anyone not familiar with the books, they are middle grade/young adult fantasies that take place at a magical boarding school. The titular character is a teenage boy who is a Chosen One hunted by the evil Lord Voldemort and his agents. His best friends,

Ron Weasley and Hermione Granger, help him thwart the villains in each book by solving an elaborate mystery. Thus, the genre is boarding school fantasy/mystery.

The main vehicle for kishōtenketsu in *Prisoner of Azkaban* is the plot thread regarding Hermione's busy academic schedule. Each recurrence of this plot thread is actually working on many levels at once:

1. It establishes Hermione's ambitiousness as an affectionate running joke.

2. It suggests a mysterious secret mission Hermione is obsessed with (possibly regarding escaped murderer Sirius Black).

3. It highlights the growing emotional rift between Hermione and her two best friends, Harry and Ron, as Hermione matures faster than they do.

4. It feeds into the plot of Professor Snape's poisoning of Professor Lupin.

And then, when the big twist is revealed, you realize that those four things were all decoys for the real purpose of the plot thread.

The twist is that Hermione has actually been using a time-turner, a heavily regulated device that allows her to travel back in time. She has been using it to pack her academic schedule and take all the classes she wants, even if they are scheduled at the same time. She uses it to go back in time and resolve various plot threads. Note how the third-act new element changes the story from a straight-up fantasy into a science fiction story, and a very clever one at that. While magic, magical creatures, and other features of fantasy continue to figure in the book, the plot jumps genre rails and focuses on the particular delights of time-travel stories.

Note that the third-act new element occurs around the eighty-percent mark in the book. Thus, it is located somewhat later than the third-act element in classic kishōtenketsu, but remember that the act lengths don't have to be uniform.

This is a self-fulfilling, closed-loop time-travel story, not one with branching multiverses. The crowded fourth act does a truly astonishing job of harmonizing by showing how all the elements that came before had an unseen relationship with each other and looped back on themselves. This applies not just to Hermione's busy academic schedule, but also to the central mysteries of the story, including those surrounding Sirius Black, Professor Lupin's secret, the fate of the hippogriff Buckbeak, the Marauder's map, what became of Peter Pettigrew, and so on. Each of the pieces had previously held its own coherent and recognizable shape and stood on its own legs. In the fourth act, they snap together and magically interlock to form a larger shape. The storytelling choreography required to pull off such a trick is remarkable.

Thus, *Prisoner of Azkaban*, like the Nintendo games, serves as proof that the four-act structure is not too strange or inaccessible for Western audiences.

ACT TWO

Circular/Nested Story Structures

CIRCULAR/NESTED STRUCTURES

Let's now turn from the four-act structure and look at nonlinear structures, specifically circular and nested structures, many of which come from Eastern traditions. These forms achieve some interesting effects that more linear stories can't.

Circular stories often revisit the same or similar events or locations. This can involve the same characters repeating various actions or doing things that echo other events in the story. Or perhaps they revisit the same or similar events for more metaphysical reasons, such as exploring multiverses. Whatever the reason, such stories feature passages that "rhyme" with other passages. This rhyming allows authors to employ thematic stacking, embrace moral complexity, and synthesize between form and content to explode the idea that a straight line is always the most satisfying way to tell a story.

Nested storytelling is similar to circular storytelling. However, the stories do not have to revisit the same event from multiple angles starring the same characters. They can involve different events that star different characters, but these events are united by their structure (e.g., stories told within stories told within stories) and/or thematic motifs.

Let's autopsy the story "Spring, Summer, Asteroid, Bird" as an example of circular storytelling:

Multiple, standalone sections
- Four sections: spring, summer, asteroid, bird
- Each section forms a self-contained vignette

Same characters revisited
- Chelsea, a small avian theropod dinosaur (aka bird)
- Marilyn, a large theropod dinosaur (a tyrannosaur)

Same location revisited (a fig tree where Chelsea laid her eggs and that Marilyn likes to rub against)
- The original tree is located in southern Montana
- After 65 million years, a similar fig tree is located in southern Montana

Same theme revisited (survival of the fittest)
- Chelsea tries to survive in a world where she is one of the smallest creatures
- Marilyn's survival seems assured, as she is an apex predator
- The arrival of the asteroid jeopardizes the survival of both characters

Different times (including a sixty-five-million-year time jump)
- The true winner in the rivalry between Chelsea and Marilyn is not apparent until time has passed on this grand scale
- The revisiting of the same rivalry between Chelsea and Marilyn in the same location reveals new relationship dynamics

The main effect of the circular structure is that we see that no individual creature or single event matters as much as entire species' bloodlines over eons of evolution. The truth of that would have been impossible to convey with a story that only featured, say, one section focused on one encounter between Chelsea and Marilyn. Here, we get a better sense of the scope of their sixty-five-million-year grudge and who triumphed in the end.

There are many precursors to today's circular and nested stories. Many of the most famous novels in the history of East Asian literature feature episodic or loosely plotted structures with repeating events and recurring motifs, novels that aren't in a rush to advance a central linear plot. These include *The Tale of Genji*, *Journey to the West*, and *Outlaws of the Marsh* (aka *The Water Margin*). *Journey to the West* is largely composed of self-contained episodes featuring a fantastical creature or adventure that feels very similar to the "creature of the week" structure common in episodic animated or science fiction/fantasy television shows. Some would argue that the Indian epics the *Ramayana* and the *Mahabharata* are precursors as well, given their vast casts of characters and epic storylines composed of individual segments that often revisit similar themes and situations. However, so much has already been written in English about these two masterpieces by people far more learned than I, so I'll refrain from discussing them at length.

THE STORY OF THE STONE

O ne of the most famous historic precursors of modern circular and nested stories is *The Story of the Stone* (aka *The Dream of Red Mansions* or *Dream of the Red Chamber*), written by Cao Xueqin and completed after his death by Gao E based on Cao's notes and drafts. *The Story of the Stone* is often called the greatest of all Chinese novels. While it is loosely linear in that it slowly progresses with fits, starts, and delays along a chronological path, its priority is in exploring the interconnected tales of hundreds of characters, rather than pursuing a plot line from start to finish.

The book is a sprawling work about life in a declining noble household during the Qing dynasty. It defies easy characterization. It contains over three hundred characters, and the English edition, translated by David Hawkes and John Minford, comes in at 2,339 pages, not counting the supplementary materials such as lists of characters and family trees.

The book starts with a fantastical element. Long ago, the goddess Nü-Wa created many thousands of stones to repair the sky. After the repairs were done, one stone was left over. A Taoist priest encounters the stone and finds a very long story inscribed on it of its life as a mortal boy, which is the very book we are reading. The priest copies down the story and seeks a publisher for it. In a metafictional touch, the book claims that a certain Cao Xueqin spends ten years organizing and rewriting it for publication.

The bulk of the story follows Baoyu ("Precious Jade"). He is the scion of the noble Jia family and was mysteriously born with a jade in his mouth. He has been pampered his whole life. He is deeply drawn to girls and women and has a great tenderness for them.

Baoyu has a cousin named Baochai ("Precious Virtue"). She is a paragon of feminine virtue: beautiful, kind, patient, tactful, empathetic, demure. Baoyu is very fond of Baochai.

Baoyu has another cousin named Daiyu ("Black Jade"). Daiyu has been left motherless and is brought into Baoyu's household out of pity. Daiyu is wanly beautiful, chronically ill, extraordinarily sensitive, easily hurt, and often dramatic. However, Baoyu's own sensitive heart is deeply moved by this fragile, unhappy girl.

Eventually, the family leaders decide that it is in everyone's best interest for Baoyu to marry his sweet-natured cousin Baochai. However, Baoyu's heart belongs to his delicate, difficult cousin Daiyu. The leader of the family tricks Baoyu into marrying Baochai by telling him that it is Daiyu under the bridal veil. When Daiyu learns about this, she is overcome with loneliness, anger, and grief. She falls ill and dies.

Daiyu's death causes Baoyu to lose his mind with sorrow. He ultimately renounces worldly ties and the sorrows of mortal existence and disappears to become a monk.

The Story of the Stone is linear in that it follows the story of this noble family, centering on the love life of its scion Baoyu. However, the book has a circular/nested flavor to it. The book follows this vast household through many dramas, ranging from romantic rivalries, affairs, and intrigues to deaths, suicides, and scandals. Many of the events, including tragic twists of fate, have echoes and counterparts in other passages in the book, and many of the passages rhyme with each other. For example, Baoyu and Baochai both have mysterious jades with words carved on them that unaccountably and spookily complement each other. Yet, Baoyu and Daiyu also share a connection that is both spiritual in their tenderness for each other and cosmic in the overlap in their names, "Precious Jade" and "Black Jade." Characters' choices, mistakes, and destinies echo other characters' choices, mistakes, and destinies. The book's structure has been called kaleidoscopic, because of its repetitions, inversions, and refractions.

Further, the book plays metafictional games, hundreds of years before metafiction was officially invented, by making the author a character, having the Taoist priest be both the discoverer of the stone's story and the vehicle by which it came to us, having Baoyu be both a magical stone and a mortal boy, and so on. We do chart, in a loosely linear way, the dramas and decline of this noble family over many years, but characters and events mirror each other, repeat, and are reborn in new form so many times that it ultimately takes on a circular/nested feel.

RASHOMON

The film *Rashomon*, directed by Akira Kurosawa, is one of the most acclaimed and influential films of all time due to its dismantling of linear narrative and its use of multiple narrators, many of whom are unreliable. It is perhaps the most iconic example of circular storytelling, so well-known that the term "Rashomon effect" is used in psychological and legal contexts to discuss subjectivity and the unreliability of witness testimony.

Rashomon takes place in eleventh-century Japan. A woodcutter and a priest are sheltering from a rainstorm in the remains of the Rashomon gatehouse in Kyoto. A commoner joins them. The woodcutter and the priest have just testified as witnesses at an unusual murder trial.

The woodcutter tells the commoner of finding the body of a samurai as well as discarded personal articles and a cut rope, which we see as enacted footage, as if we had witnessed the occurrence ourselves. He alerts the police and testifies at trial about what he saw, which we also see as though it had happened. He is asked if he found a sword at the scene, and he says no. Although we do not have any indication yet that the woodcutter might be lying, it is important to remember that the events we are seeing happen are actually just the woodcutter's account, which might be unreliable.

We then see a scene in which the priest testifies at trial. However, we do not cut back to a scene of the priest telling the commoner about his testimony at trial, so this is presumably still the woodcutter's account to the commoner of the priest's testimony at trial, adding another layer of unreliability. The priest testifies about crossing paths with the samurai shortly before his death, which we also see as if it had happened. The samurai was wearing his sword and carrying his bow and arrows as he escorted his veiled lady on a horse. The priest could not see the lady's face, as it was obscured by the veil.

The policeman appears in court with the bandit tied up. This is still presumably within the woodcutter's account to the commoner. We see the policeman's testimony at court about how he found the bandit, whom he recognized, with the same sword and bow and arrows that he had previously seen him with. The policeman then recounts how he found the bandit, a scene that we get to witness. He found the bandit lying on a shore after being thrown off his horse and injured. He found him with the bow, arrows, and horse stolen from the samurai. Back in court, the policeman says it was ironic justice that the bandit should be thrown by a stolen horse.

The bandit laughs and claims that is not how things happened. The bandit recounts his tale. We also see the bandit's account as if it had happened, although it is actually the bandit's account as heard by the woodcutter as told to the commoner, so there are multiple levels of possible unreliability built in. The bandit claims that the horse was his and that he got off the horse in a field, not by a shore, to relieve himself and then take a nap. The samurai and his veiled lady passed by. He glimpsed the lady's face behind the veil and resolved to ravish the woman without killing the samurai, if possible.

He overpowered the samurai and tied him up. He attempted to ravish the woman in front of her husband. At first, she ferociously fought back, but eventually she relented and willingly gave herself to the bandit. After, she said that either the bandit or the samurai must die. She could not bear to have her shame known by two men. She agreed to go with the survivor. The bandit cut the samurai free and handed him his sword. The bandit fairly beat the samurai and slew him. The bandit states that the woman fled during the fighting, that he took the samurai's sword, and that he exchanged it in town for liquor.

Back at the Rashomon gate, we return to the main "frame tale" surrounding the various accounts. The commoner replies to the woodcutter that he has heard the reputation of this bandit. The priest then chimes in to say that the woman was found by police and testified at trial. The woodcutter cuts in to claim that both the bandit and the woman lied at trial. The priest declares that because of human weakness, people lie, including to themselves.

The priest proceeds to claim that the woman was far from the fierce and spirited creature that the bandit reported. He claims that she was docile and pitiful at trial. We then see the scene of the woman's testimony at trial. She proceeds to recount the scene, which we see as if it happened, although this is the woman's testimony as reported in the priest's account, so there are two layers of unreliability. The woman testifies tearfully about being raped by the bandit in front of her husband. Then we see that the bandit left the woman and the samurai, cackling at their humiliation. The woman crawled to her husband. He stared at her with loathing. She retrieved her knife, cut him free, and demanded that he kill her rather than continue to look at her with such contempt. He continued to stare at her coldly. Unable to bear his disgust, she approached him with the knife. She testifies that she must have fainted and when she came to, she found her dagger in her husband's chest. She claims to have tried to commit suicide but failed.

Back at the Rashomon gate, the priest tells the commoner that the dead samurai himself testified at the trial through a medium. The woodcutter claims that this testimony was also a lie.

The medium appears at trial, which we see enacted, presumably reported through the priest to the commoner. She speaks with the voice of the samurai, claiming to be in hell. We see enacted the account of the samurai, speaking through the medium, as reported by the priest, about what happened after the bandit raped the samurai's wife. The bandit urged the woman to leave her husband and go with him since her husband wouldn't have her now that she was "tainted." The woman agreed but demanded that the bandit kill her husband. The bandit was repulsed by the woman's disloyalty and asked the samurai what he wanted him to do to her. The woman broke away and fled. The bandit was unable to catch her. He cut the samurai free and departed. The samurai, broken by his wife's faithlessness, retrieved her dropped dagger and stabbed himself. At the trial, the samurai testifies through the medium that someone came along and removed the dagger from his heart.

Back at the Rashomon gate, the woodcutter paces. He calls the testimony false and insists that the samurai was killed by a sword, not a dagger. The commoner suspects that the woodcutter saw more than he testified about and urges him to tell them now. The woodcutter admits that he didn't come across the slain samurai. He happened upon a scene of the samurai tied up. In front of him was his wife crying and the bandit on his knees begging for her forgiveness. We see the woodcutter's account enacted. The bandit pleaded with the woman to be his wife, promised to reform his ways, and threatened to kill her if she said no. The woman grabbed her dagger, ran to her husband, and cut him free. The bandit prepared to fight the samurai for the woman.

However, the samurai refused to fight, saying he would not risk his life for such a tainted woman. He told her she should kill herself and told the bandit that he could have her. The woman then turned to the bandit, wordlessly pleading for him to take her. He was repulsed by her fickleness and spurned her now as well. The woman called them both petty and cowardly for refusing to fight over her. The men were spurned into defending their masculinity, and they dueled. The fighting was surprisingly undignified, with much flailing, crawling on the ground, clamoring up hillsides and sliding back down, falling and not being able to get back up, and throwing of dirt in each other's faces. The samurai died in a particularly un-samurai-like way, disarmed, scrambling backward on all fours through the dirt and leaves, and protesting at the end that he didn't want to die. The woman fled and the bandit left the scene with both swords.

Back at the Rashomon gate, the commoner doubts the woodcutter's account of what really happened, claiming the impossibility of knowing what is within people's hearts because people all lie for their own reasons. The priest refuses to believe that there is so little goodness in the world.

They hear a mewling sound nearby. They discover an abandoned baby, wrapped with a kimono and an amulet. The commoner discards the baby but pilfers the kimono and amulet it was left with. The woodcutter berates him for his selfishness and greed. The commoner calls the woodcutter a hypocrite. He says that the woodcutter might have fooled the court, but it's clear that it was the woodcutter who stole the woman's valuable pearl-inlaid dagger from the scene of the crime. The revelation disgusts the priest, who teeters on losing all faith in humanity.

However, the woodcutter takes the baby, offering to raise it with his own six children. The priest's faith in the goodness of people is restored, even if that goodness exists beside darkness and greed.

Rashomon's radical, nonlinear story is one of the most famous examples of the circular structure. We revisit the same events multiple times, starring the same characters but told from the viewpoints of different characters. The differences are subtle but significant. This circular structure supports the exploration of a number of themes:

1. Truth cannot be ascertained from a single telling or from a single viewpoint, no matter how rigorous the scrutiny of that telling or viewpoint.

2. Only multiple passes at the same subject matter can ultimately reveal truth.

3. Multiple passes do not just reveal the subject matter in greater detail, they clarify the relationships among the people involved.

4. An understanding of the relationships among the people involved is at least as important as the subject matter itself.

Let's consider some of the storytelling craft lessons contained in *Rashomon*:

1. Circular stories revisit the same subject matter, but the multiple passes are not wasted because they are not identical.

2. The multiple passes are opportunities for development of characters and character relationships, not just straightforward plot progression.

3. The multiple passes also offer the chance to travel deeper (vertically) rather than along a plot line (horizontally).

4. Circular stories create opportunities for storytellers to embrace complexity in their characters' motivations, thoughts, and understanding.

The circular structure thus unmoors the story from a sole hero's or protagonist's viewpoint. The relationships among the various characters matter more than any single individual. The community's interactions and dynamics are the focus.

There are filmic choices that accentuate these effects. For example, note how deliberately artificial most of the scenes in the film are. The enactments subvert our habit of believing that what we see filmed is truth. Even though it's "happening" before our eyes, the falseness of the performances reminds us to proceed with skepticism. The film reminds us that what we are watching is acting, but then so is any account to some extent. Further, the music is remarkably similar to Ravel's *Boléro*. This underscores the subtext that dueling truths among various witnesses with different motivations is not just posturing, it is a dance.

THE MERCHANT AND THE ALCHEMIST'S GATE

Nested storytelling is similar to circular storytelling, but it doesn't have to feature multiple visits to the same events or multiple scenes starring the same characters. It can instead comprise stories featuring different events or characters that are connected in other ways.

The Merchant and the Alchemist's Gate is a dazzling example of the structure. This novelette by Ted Chiang is included in his collection *Exhalation*, a book that belongs in every speculative fiction reader's library. Chiang writes infrequently and writes only short fiction. However, he is one of those rare writers who produces only works that are utterly essential reading. *The Merchant and the Alchemist's Gate* is one of his greatest achievements, a time-travel story infusing a *Thousand and One Nights* fantasy. The story follows characters in medieval Baghdad and Cairo in a series of interconnected tales as they travel backward or forward in time through a portal created by alchemy. The story won both the Nebula Award and the Hugo Award, the two most prestigious science fiction and fantasy awards, for best novelette.

Frame Tale (told by merchant to caliph)

In Baghdad, a merchant tells the caliph of how he met an alchemist who showed him various gates that allow for travel through time and who told him various tales of people who traveled through the gates.

Tale One: The Tale of the Fortunate Ropemaker (told by the ropemaker Hassan to alchemist to merchant to caliph)

Poor young ropemaker Hassan travels through a gate to visit his older self. His older self gives him advice to make him prosperous and tells him the location of a buried treasure. Older Hassan explains that when he was a young man, he traveled through the gate to visit his own older self, who also told him about the treasure, in a seemingly infinite chain extending endlessly backward. Heeding his older self's advice, Hassan lives well and marries a good woman.

Frame Tale (told by merchant to caliph)

The merchant tells the caliph that he asked the alchemist if the gate can be taken advantage of by profiteering people or whether fate only allows the prudent through the gate. The alchemist told the merchant a cautionary tale about abusing the gate.

Tale Two: The Tale of the Weaver Who Stole from Himself (told by the weaver Ajib to alchemist to merchant to caliph)

When Ajib the weaver hears of Hassan the ropemaker's success in going through the gate, he goes through the gate hoping to meet his own wealthy older self. He finds his older self living in a shabby style but with a chest of unspent gold. He "borrows" the gold from his own miserly older self. He then returns to his own time, marries a woman he desires, and lives large. However, robbers see their lavish lifestyle and kidnap his wife Tahira. Ajib gives away the remainder of his money to ransom back Tahira. When Tahira learns that Ajib "borrowed" the money from someone else to pay for their wedding and her ransom, she insists that they work and save money to someday pay it back. When Ajib is an old and bitter man, his own younger self finally comes to "borrow" the money, again in a seemingly infinite chain extending endlessly forward.

Frame Tale (told by merchant to caliph)

The merchant tells the caliph that the alchemist then told him that the wife of Hassan the ropemaker (from Tale One) told him another tale that ran underneath her husband's tale.

Tale Three: The Tale of the Wife and Her Lover (told by Hassan's wife Raniya to alchemist to merchant to caliph)

Hassan's wife Raniya sees older Hassan with a young man who looks like him. She recognizes the young man as Hassan's younger self. Struck by his youthful beauty, which she had forgotten, and remembering their youthful passion, Raniya is besotted. She had always been a faithful wife, but here was a chance that would never come again to satisfy her desire with this younger man while not actually being unfaithful to her husband. When older Hassan is out of town, she goes back in time and finds the younger Hassan. She discovers that younger Hassan is in trouble with robbers whose treasure the Hassans collectively found because of a necklace Hassan was trying to sell that the robbers recognized as theirs. Raniya travels to the future to fetch her own future self, and with her future self's help and the two duplicates of the necklace, they are able to save Hassan. She then seduces younger Hassan but finds that, contrary to her memory, he is a terrible lover. Then she realizes that he was a good lover when they met only because her older (present) self had taught him. So she trains him in the ways of love in preparation for the day when he would meet her younger self.

Frame Tale (told by merchant to caliph)

The merchant tells the caliph that Tale Three, the tale of Hassan's wife, affected the merchant in ways that the first two didn't. He tells the caliph that he understood, after hearing that third story, that the past is unchangeable but that it is possible for us to know past and future more fully than we usually do. He told the alchemist that he was ready to go through the gate. He didn't want to go to the future but to the past.

However, that gate had only been built the week before, so it couldn't go further than a week into the past. The alchemist said that there was an older gate in Cairo that would allow for travel much further into the past, but the alchemist warned that the past cannot be changed. The merchant traveled to Cairo and went to the past.

Tale Four: The Merchant's Tale (told by merchant to caliph)

Many years earlier, the merchant had a kind, wonderful wife. The merchant had the opportunity to profit by selling slaves, but his wife was against it. They quarreled; he spoke harshly to her. He went on a business trip, and while he was away, the wall of a mosque collapsed, injuring his wife. A few days later, before he returned, she died. The merchant freed the slaves he had bought, and he continued living in grief and guilt. For the past twenty years he has been repenting and atoning, but he is still broken. However, Raniya's tale (Tale Three) gives him hope. He wonders if maybe there had been a mistake, and it was another woman who was killed. This is his reason for returning to the past.

In the Cairo of twenty years previous, the merchant meets the younger alchemist, who of course doesn't remember the merchant. The merchant asks the alchemist if he has ever thought of opening a shop in Baghdad. The alchemist says no, but the knowledge the merchant brings of the alchemist's future shop in Baghdad plants the seed of an idea to expand to Baghdad someday. The merchant tries to travel to Baghdad to meet his wife before she dies. Due to various calamities, he arrives too late and receives the worst news of his life a second time. However, a woman had heard his wife's deathbed words. His wife had sent the woman to look for the merchant. The woman tells the merchant that his wife had forgiven him before she died. The knowledge gives the merchant peace at last.

Frame Tale (told by merchant to caliph)

The merchant tells the caliph that after the woman told him about his wife, he wandered the streets of Baghdad, and at first the city's guards detained him, but because he came from the "future," he remembered things before they happened. By proving such knowledge, the merchant was given permission to be brought before the caliph to relay this wondrous tale—the one he is currently telling the caliph.

The structure of this story allows for some unusual effects. First, the structure is very reminiscent of *The Thousand and One Nights*, which will be discussed at length later in this book. Chiang has said that he chose a *Thousand and One Nights* structure because those stories arose largely from the Muslim world. The idea of fate is important in Islam, and that storytelling tradition lent itself to a time-travel story that rigorously played with fate and free will.

Nested stories are different from circular stories in that they don't necessarily revisit the same events multiple times with the same characters. Nonetheless, nested stories often have a roughly circular shape in that they loop in on themselves. This aspect of the nested storytelling form is present in *The Merchant and the Alchemist's Gate* in the ways that the stories are self-fulfilling.

The story also uses this aspect of looping back on itself to make a profound comment on the paradox of fate and free will in time-travel stories. Fate and free will regularly appear as themes in such stories because the genre bends our notions of cause and effect. If you go back in time and learn that you are going to receive some bad fate, do you have any free will to prevent it? Does knowing the effect ahead of time impart any ability to alter the cause to avert the effect? Is forewarned forearmed? Or rather, do circumstances conspire against you so that your very attempt to dodge the effect ultimately and ironically delivers you to the fate you sought to avoid, Oedipus Rex–style? The converse is explored in time-travel stories as well. Does going to the future and seeing yourself alive as an old person mean that you can ride into battle knowing you are invincible because you already know you will live to be old? Where is there room for fate or free will in these tidy and impenetrable loops created by time-travel stories?

The Merchant and the Alchemist's Gate deals with the paradox regarding fate in an unusual way—the paradox is dismissed with a religious explanation. Older Hassan tells younger Hassan the location of the buried treasure; younger Hassan asks how older Hassan learned it. Older Hassan says that of course, when he was a young man, his own older self told him the location of the buried treasure. The mind reels at the seemingly infinite chain of Hassans who told their younger selves the location of the treasure. However, this can feel like sleight of hand or bootstrapping, in that an effect appears to be causing itself. How did the infinite Hassans collectively know of the location of the hidden treasure to pass this knowledge on to their own younger selves? The story answers this only by saying that it was Allah's will that they know it. That might seem like an unsatisfying answer, but it should be no more unsatisfying than answers that explain why one person is born rich but another poor, why an author chooses to give one character looks, luck, and love and deny those things to another character. What matters morally in life is what a person does with the circumstances they are handed. What is interesting in a story is the same.

The question of free will is the flip side of the question of fate in time-travel stories, and it raises similar questions about cause and effect due to the circular aspect of the genre. In this story, as with fate, the question is answered with a religious explanation. When Raniya sees that the younger version of her husband Hassan is in danger from robbers, she knows that they will not kill him because he lives to meet and marry her. However, she also cannot accept that it is Allah's will that she stand by and do nothing, and perhaps she enjoys the future she enjoys precisely because she is the kind of person who cannot stand by and do nothing. Allah must have selected her to go through the gate because he knows she is the type of person who would take action to save Hassan, and thus could be an effective agent of destiny. It is Allah's will to use Raniya's free will and resourceful personality to preserve Raniya's own destiny.

The revisiting of the themes of fate and free will through nested examples provides a more compelling argument for this worldview than any one illustration could achieve. The emotional connection that the merchant makes to elements of the stories he hears is what causes him to embark on a tale that mirrors those tales. The more stories he hears of others traveling through the gate, the more he understands the gate's wisdom. The more lessons he learns in their stories, the more he sees that he has an unfinished story himself. It is the slow exposure to the joys and sorrows of others as they take their strange journeys through the gate that ultimately inspires the merchant to face the journey he needs to take to heal a great emotional wound. The revelation and peace that he obtains through that journey lend the themes of fate and free will an emotional heft that would be hard to achieve with a simpler story told in a straight line, proceeding from A to B. The ingenuity of the story's form and our awe at its construction mimic the wonder and reverence that the characters feel in the face of destiny and the universe's construction, whether one chooses to call that Allah's will or something else.

EVERYTHING EVERYWHERE ALL AT ONCE

This beloved, bewildering, gonzo tour de force, written and directed by Daniel Kwan and Daniel Scheinert, swept the Oscars and made Asian American history on a number of fronts, including Michelle Yeoh's win as best actress, the first for an Asian actress. This story focuses on the interpersonal dynamics in an Asian American family's life. However, it explores those dynamics by diving into a dizzying array of alternate universes, where the roles and relationships of the characters are reshuffled. The film's reliance on the multiple universes exemplifies both circular and nested storytelling.

The story starts mundanely in "our" universe. Evelyn Wang owns and operates a laundromat with her husband, Waymond. They live above the laundromat with their daughter Joy. Evelyn's father Gong Gong has arrived from China to live with them.

Fissures in the relationships quickly become evident. Waymond is trying to find an opportunity to serve Evelyn with divorce papers. Evelyn is outwardly critical of her daughter Joy and is not fully accepting of the fact that Joy is gay. Gong Gong brings historical baggage in his disapproval of Evelyn's life choices. Further, the Wangs' business is undergoing a tax audit, presided over by the stern IRS agent Deirdre.

The film quickly punches eject out of these quotidian matters when Waymond's manner radically changes from mild and fearful to focused and urgent. He informs Evelyn that she is in great danger. We learn that this other version of Waymond is jacking in from another "alpha" universe that "spawned" an infinite number of increasingly different universes—including the one the characters are currently in. Alpha Waymond explains to Evelyn that every time someone makes a decision, a slightly different universe is spawned. He also explains that the two of them are being hunted.

He tells Evelyn that she is potentially the only person who can stop a powerful entity named Jobu Tupaki, who has been jumping across universes, causing death and destruction. Jobu Tupaki is specifically hunting Evelyn. In the original alpha universe, that version of Evelyn was a genius who discovered a way to communicate with the other parallel universes to allow people to access the memories and skills of their parallel selves. However, Jobu Tupaki murdered that Evelyn and is hunting for another version of Evelyn in one of the parallel universes who might also be able to stand up to Jobu. Further, Jobu has been building some weapon that is spreading chaos and corruption across all the universes.

Finally, Waymond shows our Evelyn how to access experiences and abilities from parallel selves in other universes. He helps Evelyn tap into other universes where they have awesome martial arts powers.

The film then plunges into an overwhelming array of different universes, where Evelyn, Waymond, Joy, Deirdre, and Gong Gong all have different jobs, skills, lives, experiences, identities, and/or relationships with each other. In one, Evelyn never married Waymond and became a martial arts film star. In another, the conditions for organic life never formed, and Evelyn and her daughter spent eternity as rocks beside each other. In another, human evolution switched to a track in which people had hot dog–like appendages for fingers, and Evelyn and Deirdre were lovers.

Some emotional throughlines emerge from the jumble of wildly different universes. Jobu Tupaki is in fact Joy. In the alpha universe, Evelyn began training young minds to verse-jump to connect with the other universes. The candidate with the most potential was the alpha universe version of Joy. Evelyn pushed her beyond her abilities, and Joy was crushed by Evelyn's expectations and disappointment in her. Joy's hurt caused her to crack. Her mind fractured and now exists in all possible universes simultaneously. This is the entity known as Jobu Tupaki. She has turned nihilistic and has sent her minions, including her main henchwoman Deirdre, to hunt down Evelyn. Jobu has also created a black hole in the form of a bagel with every human experience on it. She threatens to activate it and destroy everything as a way to escape her feelings of parental abandonment.

Evelyn comes to recognize that her own failures to live up to her potential sprang from Gong Gong's disapproval of her choices and his readiness to give up on her. She also comes to appreciate that Waymond is not too soft, as Gong Gong had claimed. In fact, Waymond's gentle, empathetic approach to dealing with conflict achieves connections and results that Evelyn had never been able to understand.

These revelations about the two most important relationships she has with men in her life lead Evelyn to accept her own failures to achieve her potential. This allows her to accept the same in her daughter.

Jobu activates the apocalyptic everything-bagel black hole. Across multiple universes, Evelyn refuses to allow Joy to fling herself into the bagel or to flee from her mother's embrace. Evelyn tells Joy that of all the possible places she could be and all the possible things she could be, she chooses to be here with her daughter, despite all their differences and how much they have hurt and disappointed each other. Joy retorts that there are only a few specks of time when things make sense. Evelyn responds that she will cherish these specks of time and these rare moments of connection.

Evelyn, Joy, and Waymond unite and reconcile. Soon thereafter, the family returns to meet Deirdre again at the IRS office. Their tax filing is more sufficient now, but they still have issues. Evelyn surveys the people and situation around her. It seems that nothing has changed in her life, but she appreciates the mundanity of it and the small moments of meaning, connection, and kindness.

The film's bewildering, vertiginous construction operates simultaneously as circular and nested storytelling. Several of the universes exemplify circular storytelling because they feature the same characters, but with reshuffled relationships or identities where different potentials are explored. For example, Evelyn cycles through universes where she enjoys a diverse array of jobs and talents, from movie star to opera singer to teppanyaki chef. She rummages through different universes to tap into the abilities needed to get her out of one tight situation after another, usually to combat Jobu's posse, especially Deirdre. The glimpses into Evelyn's alternate career paths are repeated so often that the circular nature of this subplot becomes a defining feature of the film.

The relationship between Evelyn and Waymond is another example of circular storytelling. In our universe, Gong Gong disapproved of Evelyn's marrying Waymond because he felt Waymond was too soft. Evelyn defied her father, married Waymond, gave birth to Joy, and now owns and operates a laundromat with Waymond. In this universe, Waymond is gentle, mousy, and conflict averse.

However, in the alpha universe, there is an entirely different Waymond who is not only bold and decisive, but a kung fu badass who pummels thugs with his fanny pack of death.

In a third universe, Evelyn did not accept Waymond's marriage proposal. While walking home alone from their breakup, Evelyn is set upon by thugs and rescued by a martial arts master. The martial arts master takes Evelyn on as a protégée. Evelyn masters martial arts and becomes an action film movie star. At a glamorous premiere of one of her movies, she bumps into the Waymond she rejected, who is now a successful businessman. They share a wistful moment of regret together. He tells her, "In another life, I would have really liked just doing laundry and taxes with you."

In what is possibly a fourth universe, one that might or might not be the original universe the film started in, Waymond's alleged softness is shown to be a great strength. He uses compassion to convince the villainous Deirdre to give them an extension on their taxes. He argues with Evelyn for the importance of kindness. In this universe, Evelyn finally appreciates the gentle, steady power in Waymond's kindness, which leads to her own breakthrough about her relationship with their daughter.

Thus, the film revisits the three elements of Evelyn, Waymond, and the nature of their relationship again and again in a circular fashion. It has the two lovers circling each other through universes, locked by destiny in a common orbit.

The film simultaneously exhibits nested storytelling. The tale of Evelyn and Waymond is braided into the tale of Evelyn and Joy, as well as the tale of Evelyn and Gong Gong and the tale of Evelyn and Deirdre. Revelations in the tales bleed into each other. In the tale of Evelyn and Waymond, Evelyn comes to appreciate the strength of kindness. This causes her to complete the tale of Evelyn and Gong Gong because of her new understanding of how her father's disapproval impacted her. This revelation in turn causes Evelyn to realize that unconditional support is what is needed to heal her relationship with her daughter in the tale of Evelyn and Joy. Meanwhile, the tale of Evelyn and Waymond causes Evelyn to realize that empathy is the key to establishing an understanding with Deirdre in the tale of Evelyn and Deirdre.

In addition, nested storytelling often uses unifying themes to bring together the various component parts of the story. Despite the whiplash turns in style, genre, and tone, the film is focused on the theme of potential. The word "potential" is generally considered to be positive and full of hope and optimism. However, it can have very negative connotations as well. For some, "potential" means the possibility of not fulfilling that potential. For others, a wide array of possibilities is not liberating but instead paralyzing. The film explores that theme, grafted onto a mother–daughter tale of a parent trying to salve their own unfulfilled potential by hammering their child with warnings not to repeat their mistakes, thus ensuring that the child will face the very same paralysis in response. The alternate universes show Evelyn her vast potential, but her "real" universe is one in which she hasn't pursued any of her goals or realized any of that potential. Her rift with Joy is due to her disappointment in her daughter's repeating Evelyn's own mistake of not realizing her full potential. This theme of potential is also present in the tale of Evelyn and Waymond and the tale of Evelyn and Gong Gong. It's even present in the background scenery of the tale of Evelyn and Deirdre. The couple's tax problems arise in part from Evelyn's taking deductions on endeavors that she considers side hustles to explore her artistic potential but that the IRS considers hobbies.

Further, the exploration of the theme of unfulfilled potential, and the paralysis that can come when facing unlimited potential, is made more convincing because we actually see that potential depicted in the multiplicity of different universes. The nested structure of universe after universe allows for a much more thorough and effective exploration of these themes than would have been possible with a more linear structure.

The circular/nested structures on display in the film are so intricate and the cinematic experience so overwhelming that it can be hard to see the core emotional and family dynamics that are its foundation. However, the complicated structure works well as a metaphor for its substantive story. It is hard for us to understand the real explanations for why we do things and the real reasons our relationships are broken when we are busy responding to the world around us. Even when the truth is obvious and simple, it can be hard to see it when we are constantly reacting to the distractions of the world, just as it is difficult for the viewer to see how simple a family story this truly is while trying to make sense of the Byzantine structure. The film thus achieves a harmonizing between form and content, creating a more impactful whole.

METROID GAMES

The critical and commercial triumphs of *Everything Everywhere All at Once* exploded notions about what an Oscar juggernaut could look like. In short, it could look like a movie made by and for geeks. Its nested structure was just one aspect of that spirit.

In fact, geekdom has been comfortable with such story structures for a long time. One of the most beloved cult video game franchises is a Nintendo series called *Metroid*. Since 1985, when the first game in the series was released, players have been experiencing circular and nested structures as a core gameplay mechanic. The *Metroid* games are a science fiction series where you play as a space-suited heroine named Samus Aran who explores alien worlds while combatting a nemesis race, a bit like Ellen Ripley in the *Alien* film series. As in the *Mario* series, you play a character who utilizes jumping, climbing, and other physical abilities to explore environments. Combat is secondary. Discovery is primary.

The *Metroid* games come in two flavors: the third-person 2D platformers, where you view yourself from the side as if you were navigating a cross-sectional ant farm; and the first-person 3D games, where you view the world from inside Samus's helmet with her own eyes.

The thing that unites all the *Metroid* games is their emphasis on repeatedly returning to an environment. You jump around until you find a cliff ledge you can't reach. You keep exploring until you find a relic that upgrades your suit to do a . . . double jump! Armed with this ability, you hurry back to the previously unreachable ledge and leap up there with your new double jump. Doing so grants you access to a space-ship environment where you see tantalizing tracks leading up the walls and crisscrossing the roofs, which would give you access to otherwise unreachable areas. However, you have no ability to ride those tracks. You continue to wander around until you eventually find a relic that allows you to curl up into a ball and magnetically roll up those tracks. You hurry back to the previous area and now gleefully roll like a pill bug up the wall and ceiling tracks in magnetic ball form.

The game keeps folding back on itself, forcing you to scour environments you pass through for features that you have to remember when their significance is retroactively revealed. It often throws new obstacles in the way, like populating a location that you previously cleared of enemies with new, tougher enemies that use unfamiliar attack patterns and have a new set of weaknesses you have to discover. You know that later, you will find the ability upgrade that will permit you to exploit a particular feature of the environment. You return to the environment and are rewarded with another environment that contains further such clues, or else it folds back yet again on a prior environment. The *Metroid* series is built entirely around this gameplay mechanic of repeating, revisiting, and reviewing an environment in a new light. *Metroid* proudly pins its circular/nested structure on its chest as one of its defining features.

This emphasis on the circular/nested structure develops and rewards powers of observation. Environments are never simply atmospheric backdrops against which to battle enemies. The environments themselves are always the true enemies to vanquish, and they can never be defeated with just brute force or even manual dexterity and hand-eye coordination. They must be conquered with puzzle-solving skills. However, the environments contain multiple levels of features that you must memorize so that you can later return and capitalize upon them. You can't notice only the currently unreachable ledge leading to some new place; you must also notice the tantalizing tracks leading to some other new place, knowing that the game will contrive to bring you back to this environment multiple times.

The subtext here is that secrets are always in plain view. This idea is central to Nintendo's game-design philosophy. Nintendo's games teach players that the world around us is filled with one discovery after another, but they're available only to those of us with a sense of curiosity. The world is perpetually wondrous only to those persistent enough to keep digging deeper and deeper to find the story within the story.

CIRCULAR/NESTED STRUCTURES IN WESTERN STORIES

The previous case studies spotlight circular and nested stories from Eastern creators and/or told in Eastern settings to demonstrate the rich tradition of such structures in Eastern storytelling. But circular and nested stories are of course far from unknown in Western culture. Modern popular examples include the film *Groundhog Day* (written by Danny Rubin and Harold Ramis, directed by Harold Ramis), the film *Pulp Fiction* (written by Quentin Tarantino and Roger Avary, directed by Quentin Tarantino), the film *Mulholland Drive* (written and directed by David Lynch), the film *Lost Highway* (written by David Lynch and Barry Gifford, directed by David Lynch), the television series *Russian Doll* (created by Natasha Lyonne, Amy Poehler, and Leslye Headland), the film *Run Lola Run* (written and directed by Tom Tykwer), the novel *Invisible Cities* (by Italo Calvino), the novel *Einstein's Dreams* (by Alan Lightman), and the video game *Returnal* (Sony Interactive Entertainment). I'd argue that stories or collections that are simply intertwined stories or anthologies of various stories, such as *The Canterbury Tales* (by Geoffrey Chaucer), don't quite count as truly circular or nested because their structures don't engage with or interact with their substantive themes in a meaningful way.

One particularly thought-provoking Western use of the circular structure is in the film *Last Year at Marienbad* (written by Alain Robbe-Grillet, directed by Alain Resnais). The film takes place in a palatial European resort. Guests in stately dress populate its drawing rooms and glide through its corridors in impassive near silence. The film revolves around three characters: a beautiful woman named "A," a dapper man named "X," and a plain man named "M" who might be A's husband and who acts possessively toward her.

As the guests move through the gestures of luxurious leisure in this sparkling chateau, X repeatedly stalks A. He corners her alone and tells her that they met last year. A insists that he must be mistaken. X tries to conjure up memories of the words and moments they shared. A says she does not remember. X reminds her of promises they made to each other. A asks him to leave her alone. X reminds her of their plan to meet in her bedroom while M is occupied with the gaming tables. She does not, cannot, or will not remember. X claims that A pleaded with him to delay his demands for one year but that she promised she would meet him here after that year had passed. We see some of these memories and it becomes hard to tell what is happening, what happened, and what is imagined.

It appears at first that X is trying to plant false memories in A, or that he is trying to rattle her faith in the reliability of her own memories. However, X himself struggles to remember things correctly. He recounts a shooting that occurred, then corrects himself and begins to feel his way toward another version of the event. He recounts M's discovering them, then not discovering them.

We are exposed to mutually incompatible enactments of various scenes. In some of them, A acts as X's lover; in some she does not. We do not know which ones are real events, which ones are memories that A will not admit, which ones are false memories that X is trying to implant. Meanwhile, the actual physical location mirrors the fracturing happening in the narrative. Corridors, rooms, statues, and other markers of the physical environment are moved about, reversed, reshuffled. Shadows fall in two directions in one setting. Continuity is left in shreds, as characters change settings and clothing from one second to another, mid-sentence, with no explanation. It becomes impossible to maintain our orientation within the chateau. Narrative, place, and time become a hopeless tangle.

The film ends with no clear answer as to what is true and what is false. Many critics have thus engaged with *Marienbad* as if it were a dismantling of linear narrative that reveals our assumptions about point of view and reliability of narrators, especially in a filmic medium. However, I posit that the film is doing something more specific and pointed and that it intimately utilizes the circular structure to support its purpose.

Tucked into the middle of the film is a scene that lasts only a second but that suggests the reason for the film's entire structure. The scene is shot from the viewpoint of someone who has entered A's private chambers. In voiceover, X recounts how he told A he would come to her room while M was down in the game room, how he found her bedroom door ajar, how he entered and closed it behind him. On the screen, we see A look up and scream.

Shortly thereafter, as X further urges A to remember, he says to A, "It was probably not by force. But only you know."

In my reading, it is clear that A was raped or sexually assaulted, probably by X, possibly by M. As a response to this trauma, A's psyche has buried parts of the memory and all the events surrounding it. Her shattered psyche is captured in the shattered linearity of the narrative. Her inner torment is mirrored in the confusion of the competing accounts of what happened and didn't happen in the film. The foundations of the story, whom she can trust in it, and its basic truths are scrambled for her because of her trauma. In this reading, it is less a story depicting rape than an attempt to capture in its very form the emotional or mental response to trauma. There is thus synthesis between the form and the substance of the story. I would guess that Robbe-Grillet and Resnais would chafe at the suggestion that their film, which relinquishes its mysteries so unwillingly, could be reduced to so simple a single reading. Nonetheless, this story of assault and the mental response to it is undeniably poured into the foundations of this shifting labyrinth.

The circular/nested structure in *Last Year at Marienbad* actually serves to focus attention on the identification of a central theme. The film is deliberately constructed of pieces that cannot all fit together. Many of its pieces are mutually exclusive. The viewer is tasked with examining and assessing the reality of each piece. This intentionally confusing task throws down a subconscious challenge to the viewer. The viewer feels an impulse to machete through the frustrating tangle of story tendrils to get at what the film is really "about." This pitches the viewer into search mode, grasping for familiar components of story, such as a uniting theme. The filmmakers here avoid overly tidy answers by burying that theme so deep within the film. The effect after such laborious digging is that the viewer who uncovers this theme feels that the reward of revelation is truly well-earned.

ACT THREE

People Aren't People

INTRODUCTION—"SHAKESPEARE IN THE BUSH"

Act one and act two of this book explore how structures from Eastern storytelling traditions are significantly different from Western structures. However, these portions of the book include multiple examples of works that have been embraced around the world, including in the West, despite being told in Eastern structures. These include Nintendo's *Mario*, *Zelda*, and *Metroid* games (which have sold a total of over a billion copies worldwide) and Oscar powerhouses *Parasite* and *Everything Everywhere All at Once*. Readers might leap from these examples of cross-cultural appeal to a blanket statement about grand concepts like the universality of "the human condition." After all, people are people the world over, right?

Well, it might have been interesting to ask American anthropologist Laura Bohannan that question. Bohannan is the author of the immortal 1966 article "Shakespeare in the Bush." The article recounts how Bohannan, believing that human nature was the same the world over, tried to tell the story of *Hamlet* to a Tiv community in southeastern Nigeria, using Tiv words and cultural analogs. Hilarity ensued. Bohannan encountered cultural differences that radically altered the Tiv's understanding of the story.

For example, the Tiv couldn't comprehend Hamlet's inner turmoil at his uncle's marrying his mother, since it was Tiv tradition for a younger brother to marry his brother's widow and raise his brother's children as his own. Further, the vision that visited Hamlet couldn't be his father's ghost, since the Tiv didn't know what ghosts were, and they insisted that it must be an omen sent by a witch. When Bohannan said that it wasn't an omen sent by a witch but was truly Hamlet's dead father, they realized what she was talking about. They explained that in the Tiv language, the word for a person who returns from the dead is "zombi." Bohannan maintained that there were no zombies in *Hamlet*, but was forced to make change after change in her telling to accommodate the Tiv's interpretation. The story that finally limped across the finish line bore zero resemblance to *Hamlet* and satisfied no one.

CULTURAL ARROGANCE

Joseph Henrich has served as a professor of psychology at the University of British Columbia and as a professor of human evolutionary biology at Harvard. Henrich has written about the phenomenon in the field of psychology of studying only subjects from what he calls "WEIRD" (Western, Educated, Industrialized, Rich, and Democratic) societies but generalizing those findings to all of humanity. The volunteers in psychological studies are often from extremely narrow slivers of the world population. For example, between 2003 and 2007, in the prestigious *Journal of Personality and Social Psychology*, 67 percent of total experiment subjects studied in the published papers were themselves United States psychology students.[3]

Other studies have examined how this sample bias produces results that ignore the fact that culture matters and influences how people perceive and act, as well as how people wish to engage with their psychological needs. Cultural bias might map Western psychological concepts of shame onto values in other cultures, such as face, caste, or honor, that are far from direct equivalents. For example, some mental health professionals believe that the Chinese equivalent of anorexia is fundamentally different from the Western conception of anorexia because the Chinese equivalent does not necessarily focus on a fear of fatness. Displacing culturally specific concepts with Western concepts can lead to misdiagnosis and/or mistreatment. This misidentification further leads to the imposition of Western solutions. For example, populations in places such as Sri Lanka or Rwanda that have suffered natural disaster, genocide, or other mass trauma have often been funneled into individual sessions with psychiatrists instead of being allowed to process their grief communally, as tradition dictates. These populations' culturally specific notions of trauma and the strategies used to cope with it were painted over with Western substitutes.[4]

Thus, Western psychology purports to study behaviors and experiences that are universal to all humanity. However, much of Western psychology is based on limited studies done on statistically unrepresentative populations in Western countries. The notion that Western psychology's diagnoses and remedies are applicable to all people regardless of their cultural background, and that Western values should overrule other cultures' values and traditions, is an example of cultural arrogance.

INDIVIDUALISM VERSUS COLLECTIVISM

One of the significant ways that cultures differ is with regard to individualism versus collectivism. Many stories published in the West focus on themes surrounding individualism, especially in contemporary children's literature. Manifestations include themes of self-empowerment, self-esteem, "finding" or "being true to" yourself, "believing in" yourself, "owning your power," and so on. The bias is so ubiquitous that it can be hard to find a contemporary middle grade or young adult novel that isn't about at least one of these themes.

There are obvious reasons for this emphasis. These stories are nourishing for people, especially for members of marginalized communities. These stories can stabilize, improve, and even save lives. However, it is important to understand that this focus on individualistic stories is not universal across cultures, nor is it without its downsides. Psychologists have examined the phenomenon in which greater focus on individualism can lead to greater loneliness. Just look up "psychology individualism loneliness" and you'll find a wealth of articles exploring this issue. America is a proudly individualistic culture but also one with significant mental wellness issues. Those two phenomena are not unrelated. As psychotherapist James McLindon states,

In Western cultures, especially in the USA, individualism is stressed as a fundamental value, in contrast to Asian cultures where collectivism is embraced. In an individualistic society, the individual is conditioned to be autonomous, independent, and self-sufficient, and any trait that gives the appearance of being dependent, vulnerable, or lower in status is shamed and shunned. This stance of hyperindependence can often be so integrated into the individual's sense of self that it may be maintained even when it is not helpful to do so, such as refusing to ask for support from others when required. Other potential pitfalls include a sense of isolation, due to their inability to be vulnerable and open up to others, and shame when confronted with their own natural, healthy neediness. In fact, if the individual perceives another person to be needy or dependent, that shame may be projected onto that person or group of persons as anger and contempt. As a result of this disconnection from others and from the self, the individual can experience anxiety and depression.[5]

There is another unforeseen effect of this overemphasis on individualism that results from constantly telling children that they are special. We should pause and ask if we are using the correct word.

When we tell children that they are "special," we want them ideally to focus on the takeaway that they are valued. However, what children likely hear in the overuse of the word "special" is that they will be singled out, receive distinctions, and be publicly applauded. This disjunction creates problems. Not every child can be the best in their class or chosen first on a sports team or given the lead role in the school play. What do we do to children's sense of themselves when we are constantly pounding into them the importance of being special and our need for them to satisfy that expectation, but they themselves are failing every popular societal metric of specialness?

I don't feel that we as a society talk enough about how this insistence on being special can warp minds. We don't talk about the idea that maybe being good or kind is more important than being special and that perhaps we should choose our words more carefully when we're speaking to children. There is also much discussion in twenty-first-century culture about whether such obsession with specialness tends to create self-absorbed or narcissistic children. How many of the world's autocrats or dictators consider themselves special? How many more such special people can the world possibly need or tolerate? What kind of model do these people serve as for children?

The majority of books for young people produced in early twenty-first-century America fixate on this theme of being special in part because that theme is considered nutritive by gatekeepers such as parents, teachers, and librarians—the people who decide which books to press into kids' hands. For some kids, books with that theme are exactly what they need to build a sense of wholeness. Some kids will spit them out as overly medicinal. And some kids will extract from these books a message that deforms their expectations about how to measure their own value, or about what the world owes them.

An interesting analog exists in women's history. Laurel Thatcher Ulrich is a Pulitzer Prize–winning historian specializing in early America and the history of women. She is famous for coining the line "Well-behaved women seldom make history." This line has been taken up as a rallying cry and has risen to the level of T-shirt and coffee-mug aphorism. It is widely read as a call to break with tradition, to take bold action, to be special.

However, Ulrich explains in her 2007 book *Well-Behaved Women Seldom Make History* that she was in some ways trying to say the exact opposite.[6] History overlooks, undervalues, and denigrates the contributions of "good" or "domestic" women who make meaningful and consistent contributions to society but who are ignored because they are quieter. History instead *only* pays attention to those women who defy convention in showy ways. It romanticizes and glorifies the women who conform to a male model of attention-grabbing, individualistic achievement and who emulate the contributions of men as perpetuated by the myth of the Great Man (i.e., history is made by rare visionary, solitary men, not groups of people acting collectively). The original intent of Ulrich's quote was thus exactly the opposite of how it is normally used. It is also another example of the particular American fetishization of individualism and specialness.

In contrast, Asian cultures, particularly East Asian cultures, tend to emphasize collectivism more than individualism. Researchers in psychology have studied how notions of things as seemingly fundamental as self-esteem are *not* universal across cultures. Confucian culture has had far-reaching impacts, at least in East Asian and Southeast Asian countries. Since Confucianism emphasizes collectivism and interdependent self-construal, concepts from Western psychology such as "self-esteem" need to be refined. According to scholars K. S. Yang and L. Lu, who have researched the concept of Chinese self-esteem, "Self-evaluations from others, relationships, reputation, authority, family, and group are also parts of the structure of Chinese self-esteem, besides individual self-esteem."[7] A culturally aware definition of self-esteem in such Asian cultures allows for elements outside of the individual self to help construe self-esteem.

It is important to note that this book does not make a value judgment on the superiority of one set of values over another. Any sharper elbows directed at Western values are a reflection of the fact that most of this book's readers will have spent their lives in a Western value system and thus might need more assistance getting up from the comfort of that particular seat. There are certainly very dark sides to Asian collectivism. The focus on community and interconnectedness can also mean a lack of proper respect for the individual. This is particularly exacerbated when it intersects with Asian stigma regarding mental illness and prejudices against mental healthcare. I do not mean to diminish the very real and unnecessary human suffering that can result from an overemphasis on collectivism.

I am interested instead in how the difference in values manifests in the arts. Take for example the speech given by Daniel Kwan when he and Daniel Scheinert won the Academy Award for Best Directing in 2023 for *Everything Everywhere All at Once*—a speech that psychiatrist Ravi Chandra called "the most Asian American thing ever heard at the Oscars."[8]

In it, Kwan acknowledged his immigrant parents. He talked of inheriting his love of movies from his father, for whom movies were an escape from the world. He thanked his mother, who could not afford the luxury of pursuing her dancing, acting, and singing dreams, but who passed her creative spirit on to him. Kwan raised his parents as examples of the idea that genius is not the product of the individual who gets celebrated with an award. It is the product of the collective. That collective can include one's heritage and ancestors.[9]

These fundamental differences in values often manifest as fundamental differences in story themes. Traditional Western storytelling themes center primarily on the development of the individual. That's an epic generalization and I hate speaking in generalizations, but I've been doing it all throughout this book, so why stop now? Western storytelling emphasizes these themes:

1. Rising self-esteem/empowerment arc

2. Individual heroism

3. Struggle against external foes

4. Characters changing

In contrast, traditional Asian storytelling, particularly East Asian storytelling, emphasizes very different themes:

1. The relationship of the individual to the larger group (family, society)

2. Group heroism

3. Internal struggle

4. Characters understanding something within or outside of themselves

These differences are most baldly visible when two cultures take on the same story, as we will see in the next section.

SURFACE DIVERSITY

The difference between the traditional Chinese folk tale "Mulan" and the Disney animated version is an enlightening example of how different cultural values influence what story themes are considered satisfying. The Disney animated version is also a classic example of what I call "surface diversity"—in this case, a wholly Western story dressed up in Eastern drag.

In the original folk tale and poem, Mulan is a young woman who loves her family. She agrees to enlist in the army in her father's place because he is too elderly to fight. She does this not to rebel against her family or her obligations to them, but in fact to honor them. More than half of the poem is spent describing the small details of Mulan's domestic life before and after her excursion into the army. The actual war is glanced over in a few lines devoid of meaningful detail. Finally, the poem emphasizes that Mulan enjoys wearing her gowns and makeup, and the first thing she does when she returns from the war is get done up as beautifully as possible to show the soldiers she fought with that she is a girl. The original poem sets up a nonbinary notion of femininity: Mulan can both fight in a battle and wear makeup and dresses. Strength and prettiness aren't mutually exclusive. Being "girly" is not incompatible with being strong.

Disney's animated film veers wildly from these values, turning the story into a predictable Western story about rebellion against parental expectations, rejection of traditional "female" qualities and interests, physical strength, and a character's "finding herself." When the film was shown in mainland China, it bellyflopped spectacularly. The wisecracking and anachronistic humor, the flaccid jokes that worked only in English (and arguably not even then), the typical Western empowerment character arc, the rebellion against familial expectations, the emphasis on individual heroism, the sneering disdain for traditionally "feminine" qualities, and the aggrandizement of Mulan for singlehandedly saving the empire (the Emperor and all his subjects bow to her!) all make this a film that is cosmetically Chinese but 110 percent Western and contemporary in spirit. Here is an example of a project with Asian characters (and some voice actors of Asian descent) that utterly fails to understand or embrace its source culture in any meaningful way but still feels entitled to take on one of the most iconic stories in all of Asian lore. It is a perfect example of arrogance, surface diversity, formulaic storytelling, and a failure to understand fundamental cultural differences, all in one convenient place.

THE OPPOSITE OF SURFACE DIVERSITY

A number of works by writers of East Asian descent writing in English and publishing in the West defy this practice and in fact achieve the opposite of surface diversity. However, sometimes such works can be misunderstood by Western readers, especially when Eastern storytelling brushes up against Western assumptions of what constitutes a satisfying treatment of "diversity." One recent example is *The Grace of Kings* by Ken Liu, who was born in China and resides in the United States. *The Grace of Kings*, the first in his Dandelion Dynasty fantasy series, is about various struggles for control of an empire that range from interpersonal relations and betrayals to palace intrigue to epic battle sequences involving mythical beasts, vehicles, and weapons. The book is devoid of cosmetic markers of Chineseness. For example, instead of a great empire seated in a continental mass, the story takes place in the exact geographic opposite, an archipelago. The names of characters and places are invented and sound nothing like any Chinese language, and the characters' physical descriptions also subvert the assumption that this is taking place in a fantasy analog of China.

Nonetheless, *The Grace of Kings* draws deeply from Chinese lore and history. The author's deep affection for these traditions is apparent in the novel. Many of the anecdotes, lessons, moral questions, and historical or storytelling inspirations are recognizable to Chinese readers and those familiar with Chinese culture, despite the fact that the names and physical descriptions don't affirm that. For example, Liu has discussed drawing inspiration from the historical figure Lady Xuan, who ruled as regent of the state of Qin in the fourth century BCE. Liu has also acknowledged being inspired by techniques derived from Chinese oral storytelling, introducing characters in a way that imitates classic Ming dynasty novels, and approaching characterization in ways that are popular in wuxia novels. Thus, *The Grace of Kings* is a book that has a profoundly Chinese soul without having a Chinese surface. It is the opposite of surface diversity.

Further, the book is told in the four-act structure. The book centers around a bandit and a warrior in a struggle for control of the empire. In acts one and two, the bandit and the warrior unite forces and become bonded brothers. However, differences in values drive them apart until they become rivals. War seems unresolvable and peace beyond reach as the men of various factions battle each other. It is only in the second half of the story that the bandit realizes that there is a vast resource of untapped talent and fighters in the realm: the women. That surprising introduction of the women is the third-act twist. The fourth act then shows how the women's contributions have been an unseen, unappreciated treasure that ends up resolving the conflict between the two individual men. Destiny lies not in the hands of one of two great men, as it seems in the first two acts; it lies in the hands of the legions of women who are finally allowed to take their place in history.

Parasite, Everything Everywhere All at Once, and the Nintendo games we looked at earlier serve as case studies of how Eastern storytelling can get Trojan-horsed into Western audiences' hearts. However, sometimes Western audiences may choke on the shape of the story when Eastern storytelling conventions brush up against contemporary notions of diversity and the treatment of identity politics, representation, and agency. *The Grace of Kings* was criticized by many Western readers because it did not introduce the women characters as critical players in the larger war plot until the second half of the book. I assume most of these readers had never heard of the four-act structure and didn't realize that the deliberate withholding of this critical element was a feature of the story structure, rather than a shortcoming.

If the women had been foreshadowed throughout or had played prominent roles in the central conflict from the beginning of the story, the story would have been radically different. We would have been robbed of the delicious and powerful realization that the bandit leader enjoys—he had neglected half of humanity. Those who do so, do so at their own peril. Those who are humble enough to admit their oversight shall prevail. This surprising and moving twist in the story would have been utterly wrecked by a Western three-act structure that demanded the women be a major element from act one, rather than the game changer introduced in act three. The central theme of a great man's humbleness in recognizing the neglected talent of women would have been destroyed. This misunderstanding over the book's handling of women characters evidenced not a failing in the story but in the Western bias of its critics.

An even more radical example of a work that defies surface diversity, often to the objection of Western audiences, is the novel *Never Let Me Go*, by Nobel Prize–winning Japanese English author Kazuo Ishiguro. It is an even more extreme and fascinating negative image of Disney's animated *Mulan* in terms of surface diversity versus meaningful diversity. The book gets my vote for "Greatest Book of the Twenty-First Century So Far." Lev Grossman, writing in *Time* magazine, agrees.[10] The film version, written by Alex Garland and directed by Mark Romanek, is also very good, although it reorders a major revelation and puts it right in the opening intertitles.

The less said here about *Never Let Me Go*, the better. In this case, I can talk about the book without plot spoilers, although there is some discussion of themes that is spoiler adjacent.

The story follows Kathy H. and her complicated relationships with Ruth and Tommy, her two closest friends from Hailsham, a prestigious boarding school in the English countryside in perhaps the 1970s. It is told in three parts, each of which takes place in a different period of their lives. The first part of the book follows Kathy H. and her friends as children. Hailsham students are told repeatedly how special they are. The privilege they enjoy appears to be the fact that they attend Hailsham, rather than any sort of comfort or luxury, as Hailsham life appears to be fairly Spartan and ascetic. However, that is often the case at top boarding schools, at least in the United States and England. The nature of how Hailsham students are special is not fully revealed until they are well into their years at the school, and the reader is well into the first part of the book.

The second part of the book follows Kathy H. and her friends as young adults. They have graduated from Hailsham and are living together at a compound of cottages, doing farm work. The third part of the book finds them as adults. They are each doing their respective jobs. They reunite after years of separation. The way that their relationships have changed is the focus of this section.

By avoiding spoilers, I've managed to make the book sound like it is about the smallest of things. It is, on one level. Many readers bounce off the book because, like Ishiguro's *Remains of the Day*, it is focused on reading the significance in the most seemingly insignificant events and details of the characters' daily lives. The origin of a pencil case, the way one character squeezes another's shoulder, Kathy's pride in her unusually long career as a carer. The book appears to be about the smallest of things until the unveiling about what is really going on. Then, it vertiginously rockets up and suddenly reveals itself to have been about the largest things possible. It has, all along, been asking through the smallest events the most profound questions we can ask about how to construct a meaningful life.

We are examining *Never Let Me Go* because of something remarkable that the book does with regard to diversity. It is set in England and features a presumedly all-White cast. The casting of the film version confirms this presumption. However, the author was born in Japan, and the values explored in the book are deeply antithetical to those in typical Western narratives.

For example, in the face of a harsh and repressive system, the heroic thing for heroine Kathy to do is not to rise up, display individual heroism, and challenge or topple the system, but to learn to quietly bear her suffering with dignity, find peace with her place in this society, and accept her powerlessness over her destiny. The main characters come to accept their fate in sacrificing themselves for the greater societal good, and any struggle they have with the unjust system is wholly internal. Many Western readers gagged and sputtered over this life philosophy. I know people who have literally thrown this book across the room.

The triumph that Kathy, Ruth, and Tommy realize is not in changing their tragic fate; it is in finding meaning and connection despite their fate. Ishiguro has said that he considers *Never Let Me Go* to be an optimistic book. I understand that. Very few of us will ever be able to singlehandedly overturn an unjust system, regardless of how hard we work for that. Few if any of us will be able to avoid loss and suffering. However, all of us can strive to find meaning, even if we live in a far-from-perfect world, by nurturing connections with others. Stories that teach people that the only stories worth telling are ones about heroes who "win" and defeat unjust systems, dodging loss and suffering, are at best unhelpful and at worst harmful.

I'm not Japanese, but these values resonate with my own Taiwanese heritage. Ishiguro's treatment of this particular type of material is so radically different from so many Western treatments we have seen before. It is so East Asian. Yet the characters are all White and the setting is Western.

Thus, Ishiguro has done the exact reverse of what Disney's animated *Mulan* did: he has created a story with no East Asian characters that still tells a profoundly East Asian story.

Note that *Never Let Me Go* doesn't constitute "reverse" cultural appropriation of White English culture, despite the fact that it uses cosmetic trappings of a Western culture (White characters at an elite boarding school) but tells a profoundly Eastern story. The reason is that this kind of reverse cultural appropriation is a nearly impossible thing to do, at least with world history as it is currently constructed. White English culture is the dominant culture in England and is under no real threat of being underrepresented there. When a culture is dominant, it is imposed on everyone as the default, and thus there can be no fair complaint when anyone feels entitled to write about it and publish books in that country about it.

But what if this book were being published in Japan? I don't see how that makes a difference. There is no equivalent history of systemic discrimination targeting the English in Japan, at least not in recent centuries. There is, however, a long history of systemic discrimination and violence against Asians in Western countries, particularly people of Japanese descent in America, that continues to this day. People raise concerns about cultural appropriation to try to preserve a safe margin around groups that have faced erasure and suppression. For that reason, it typically doesn't run equally in both directions.

ACT FOUR

Values Dictate Structures

VALUES DICTATE STRUCTURES

Why did we just take this lengthy detour into psychology, individualism versus collectivism, and cultural values? The subtitle of this book says that it explores Eastern storytelling, not Eastern values. The reason is that this book is structured as kishōtenketsu—so you wouldn't be getting your money's worth if the third act didn't drop a random asteroid in your lap.

Of course, it's not so random after all. As an example of kishōtenketsu, the book ends with a fourth act: the harmonizing of all the elements that came before to reveal their close, though hitherto invisible, connection with each other. In fact, the four-act structure, the circular/nested structures, and the discussion of cultural values all have an intimate relationship with each other that can be summarized thus: values dictate structures.

Different story structures arise from different cultural values. The four-act structure arises from surrendering ego and will and embracing chance and change. Circular and nested structures arise from a recognition of the larger relationship, community, or history that each individual belongs to, rather than a focus on the individual. These story shapes often contain themes about sublimating the individual and exalting the relationship, community, or history. Values thus unite substance and form. There is harmony and synthesis between what a story is about and how it is structured.

The synthesis between values and structures is well-recognized in other art forms. For example, a common criticism of pre-twentieth-century Chinese architecture is that it all looks the same. However, this sameness is deliberate. Traditional Chinese architecture is intended to be modular and to reflect rank in a way that embraces Confucian principles of hierarchy. Further, the architecture reflects Chinese values of collectivism. Architecture in traditional Chinese culture is not about any individual building. It is always about a *group* of buildings. The concept even extends to the gardens connecting the buildings. Each building doesn't derive purpose from being singular and unique. It derives purpose in how it serves the larger community of buildings. The beauty resides in their placement in relation to each other as a family of structures, not just in their individual features. The beauty is the beauty of a harmonious whole. A building that is individually distinctive would interrupt that harmony and detract from the community's shared beauty.

This relationship between values and forms is not unique to Eastern cultures, of course. Christian cathedrals are laid out in a form with deep religious symbolism, with each section of the footprint representing a particular aspect of Christ or Christianity. Traditional English gardens reflect the legacy of Romanticism and individualism. Thus, they are constructed of meandering paths for lonely contemplation, a solitary oak tree atop a windswept hill, and so on. These traditional English gardens embraced pastoral naturalness in part as a response to anxieties over urbanization and industrialization. However, the English gardens were anything but natural; their creators had to go to great lengths to achieve their aesthetic effects. Oak trees do not grow alone atop a hill. They perpetually drop acorns all around them. The acorns root and must constantly be weeded out to maintain the oak's lonely posture. The lone oak is, in fact, a poser. Such are the lengths to which cultures will go to make the forms of their art reflect their values.

VALUES DICTATING FOUR-ACT STRUCTURE

Collectivist cultures, as we discussed in act three, do not prioritize the wishes of the individual over all else. They consider the surrendering of will an act of humility and personal growth. They consider the sublimation of the ego a kind of moral illumination. The reason for this is partly religious. Buddhism teaches acceptance and gratitude over desire; Taoism teaches nonaction and the relinquishing of ambition. To Westerners unfamiliar with Buddhism and Taoism, such philosophies might seem maddeningly passive.

You can probably imagine how incompatible these ideas would seem to be with much Western storytelling. A superhero movie where the superhero opts never to use their superpower. An animated musical where the teenage heroine listens to her parents and stays home. Box office poison. Many would probably say, "That's not just a bad story, that's not even a story at all," a reaction that comes from the fact that Western stories are built on tension, conflict, and the resolution of those things. But of course, as we've seen, stories without these elements can be just as satisfying.

The uniting principle in these Buddhist and Taoist ideas of collectivism and the sublimation of the ego is that an individual's will clouds their ability to see the greater design of the universe around them. Surrender of will and preconceived expectations allows us to respond with more grace, wisdom, and dignity to the unexpected events that life inevitably tosses in front of our wheels and to receive greater gifts from the universe than we would receive if we insisted on pressing forth with our own individual will. That is why the four-act structure always has a surprise third-act element. The twist gives us the opportunity to see how the character responds to an unplanned or unwelcome complication. In doing so, the character reveals their true nature. That twist also sets up the fourth act, where we're able to experience revelations about how the elements that came before are connected, connections that we might not otherwise have seen.

All of this is true of life as well. How people function in the face of disaster or the unplanned can be very telling of the nature of their hearts. Being able to observe the unseen patterns of connection in the world around us is an invaluable skill. That ability to observe is often strengthened by stillness and contemplation, which in turn are given space by a setting aside of individual will. Quietude often leads to insight and depth, while assumptions and agenda result in shallow busyness. As the Chinese aphorism goes, "Outside noisy, inside empty." Thus, the four-act structure is always a compact diorama of the rhythms of life itself, at least as seen through an East Asian cultural lens.

Let's examine the values of the story "Spring, Summer, Asteroid, Bird" and why it is told in the four-act structure. One theme it explores is that sometimes, life throws an asteroid into your plans—whether literal or metaphorical. The story explores how every catastrophe produces winners and losers and every crisis is an opportunity to reveal hidden talents.

Because of that theme, the four-act structure is the perfect way to tell this story. Chelsea is well-equipped to respond to the rapid, unscheduled merger of space material with her planet. Marilyn is not. Chelsea receives the unexpected and unwelcome element, adapts to it, and prevails. Marilyn does not. And in the process, unseen relationships—between Chelsea and Marilyn, between beaks and teeth, between seeds and meat, and between all of them and world-ending disaster—are revealed.

MY NEIGHBOR TOTORO

My *Neighbor Totoro* is a beloved 1988 animated film by Hayao Miyazaki about two young girls who move to the countryside to be near their mother, who is recuperating in a hospital. The girls discover that the woods next to their new house are inhabited by benevolent, supernatural owl-bear creature spirits. I won't spend time describing the plot in detail, as the power of the film is extremely difficult to pinpoint. Its evocation of childhood and the magic of discovery are achieved through visuals, motion, sound design, and music as much as through plot.

To appreciate how different *My Neighbor Totoro* is from just about every Disney, Pixar, or DreamWorks film, here is a list of some things that it doesn't have:

1. A villain

2. A real central conflict

3. A dead mother

4. Sibling rivalry

5. Adults who "just don't understand" or who have to be taught a life lesson by their children

6. Adults who disbelieve their children when the children report that they've encountered the supernatural

7. An empowerment character arc

8. A third-act confrontation and action sequence

In short, *My Neighbor Totoro* has none of the basic story pieces with which just about every Western animated film is built. Instead, it has the following elements:

1. Siblings who don't bicker and who like each other

2. Parents who go with the flow when their kids tell them they've encountered the supernatural and who keep an open mind about the possibility of its existence

3. Monsters that are neither frightening nor farcical

4. What might qualify in Western storytelling as a shameless final-act deus ex machina

5. Characters who don't really have flaws

6. Characters who barely change, if at all

All of this sounds like instructions for how not to write a successful story. However, the story is incredibly successful, in part because it follows kishōtenketsu and is not based on tension, conflict, and resolution.

ACT ONE—The Introduction of the Main Elements

Ten-year-old Satsuki, four-year-old Mei, and their father move to a new house near a forest.

ACT TWO—The Development of the Main Elements

The sisters explore their world and begin to go on excursions with the nearby magical creatures, the Totoros and the Catbus.

ACT THREE—The Twist/New Element

The girls learn something is wrong with their mother, and they fear she is going to die. Mei briefly becomes lost in the countryside. The tone and genre shift from lighthearted summer fantasy to family drama or story about a sick or dying loved one.

ACT FOUR—The Harmonizing of All Elements

All the characters are brought back together. Satsuki and Mei call upon the Totoros and Catbus to take them to see their mother. The fantasy plot weaves together with the domestic health-scare plot. Mother turns out to just have a cold, and she eventually recovers and comes home.

Part of the power of *My Neighbor Totoro* is that it builds a world that is wholly benevolent around Satsuki and Mei. The old house, the woods, and the spirit creatures that populate them mean the girls no harm. The movie creates a warm glow around these girls and their world in the first two acts.

When the very minor health scare comes in act three, it feels like a scorching asteroid has smashed into the girls' world. The realization that there is darkness and loss in this world is small, but the shock of it is greatly heightened because there is no gradual ramp-up to it. Things that seem small to adults can be devastating to children, and the movie's use of kishōtenketsu makes it possible for adult viewers to feel like children.

Act four sees all the elements in the story (the two children, Mom's health scare, the benevolent supernatural creatures from the nearby forest) harmonizing. The supernatural creatures from the first half of the story solve the unwelcome problem introduced in act three. The ultimate effect of this structure is that it lifts the curtain from childhood only a bit. It gives the girls only a little glimpse that unhappy things exist in this world before it drops the curtain again, telling them that they don't have to worry about that yet. Right now, the world is still a safe place, and they are allowed to be kids for just a while longer.

My Neighbor Totoro achieves these emotional effects through kishōtenketsu. If this story had a traditional Western three-act structure, the health scare would have to have been foreshadowed more heavily, in the interest of symmetry. That foreshadowing would have resulted in a more gradual ramp-up to the very minor health scare, entirely robbing it of the devastating emotional impact it has. Making the health scare more serious wouldn't have solved the problem either. The instinct of Western animated-film storytellers would probably be to "raise the stakes" by heightening the danger to the mother. However, if the threat to the mother's health or life had been more serious, the film would never have been able to convincingly return to this precious feeling of safety by the end of the story.

Like all good structures, kishōtenketsu can work simultaneously on a macro and a micro scale. Not only does the overall story of *My Neighbor Totoro* follow kishōtenketsu, many of the individual scenes within the story follow it as well. Take, for example, the sequence that shows the early part of the characters' arrival at the house, which begins just before five minutes into the film and ends just before the ten-minute mark.

ACT ONE—The Introduction of the Main Elements

Satsuki and Mei explore their rickety old house.

ACT TWO—The Development of the Main Elements

Satsuki and Mei find that nature seems to have overtaken the house, with its rotted verandah, enormous camphor tree, and acorns falling from the ceiling boards.

ACT THREE—The Twist/New Element

Satsuki and Mei unlock the bath to momentarily glimpse hundreds of mysterious black creatures.

ACT FOUR—The Harmonizing of All Elements

The girls' father comes into the room and explains that the creatures are probably soot gremlins, which you sometimes see when you go from a bright place to a dark one.

Acts one and two introduce the elements of the girls, their old house, and nature's intrusions into it. Act three tosses otherworldly black creatures into the mix. Act four harmonizes all of this by having their father explain that the black creatures are probably just a naturally occurring phenomenon in dark spaces and, in one sense, just another aspect of how nature has woven itself into the house.

In a Western animated film, this scene would probably be structured thus:

ACT ONE—Setup

Girls explore house to find ominous signs of soot gremlins.

ACT TWO—Confrontation

Girls have frightening, action-filled confrontation with soot gremlins.

ACT THREE—Resolution

Girls' father dismisses their fears as imagined, setting up for a resolution in which the girls teach their father a life lesson about the importance of believing.

Eyerolls and yawns. A Western structure would have mangled this story beyond recognition and slaughtered its sensitive, generous spirit. The film could not have achieved its effects with a structure other than kishōtenketsu.

The Buddhist/Taoist value of surrender of will is intended to silence our inner voice to allow us to better hear the voices in the world around us. In the face of an unexpected and unwelcome element, one must still the impulse to impose one's preconceptions and will onto it. Instead, one must ask what place this new thing has in the context of all things, which might lead to a revelation that presents the new thing in a different light. This idea is present in *Totoro*.

The four-act structure allows for the unexpected introduction of an unwelcome element into the girls' world, which stands in for all the hard realities of the adult world. Because of the values that inform the film, the girls are shown doing an unexpected thing in response to this unwelcome element. Instead of having to change and grow into little adults, they turn to childhood, specifically to the fantastical spirit creatures they met in the forest, for help resolving the new problem. They draw upon childish things to respond to the adult problem, and they see the creatures from the first half of the film in a new light.

A Western film would have felt obligated to steer the girls into some life lesson about growing up or learning about the world. *Totoro* instead gently urges us to let Satsuki and Mei be kids for just a little while longer. In *Totoro*, when the adult world intrudes into the safe world of childhood, the answer is to not let it change you. The answer is to call upon childhood and the connections to wondrous things that you formed there. *Totoro*'s four acts could be recharacterized as childhood, childhood, adulthood threatens childhood, childhood prevails. Childhood is the answer.

Miyazaki himself is proof of that. He is an old man with snowy hair and beard but the energy and impish mischief of a boy. He is a person with staggering talents honed in adulthood who nonetheless trains them toward capturing, uplifting, and defending the wonder of childhood. And he has deeply touched tens of millions of people because of this. Miyazaki is himself proof that childhood is the answer.

VALUES DICTATING CIRCULAR/NESTED STRUCTURES

Collectivism is a relational philosophy. It emphasizes the relationships among individuals, rather than the individuals themselves. Circular and nested story structures do the same. Circular stories show how multiple passes at the same events reveal more than any individual, linear account could, particularly with regard to the relationships among the individuals in the events and/or recounting the events. Nested storytelling allows for even grander relational networks to emerge among different individuals starring in different events, even if they have not met before. By showing commonalities and relationships among characters who might never have even met, nested storytelling attempts to chart phenomena that transcend individual experiences and constitute universal truths. In both circular and nested storytelling, the community of stories within the story is richer and truer than any individual story could hope to be.

This is true in Indian oral storytelling. In an interview with the BBC World Book Club, Salman Rushdie said that oral storytelling in Indian tradition is nonlinear. There are frequent self-interruptions with jokes, contemporary parallels, and songs, as if the storyteller were juggling several balls. Further, if the storyteller doesn't do well, people get up and leave. Rushdie urged against the advice from *Alice in Wonderland* to begin at the beginning, get to the end, and stop.[11]

This makes sense, particularly if the raw material for the story is familiar to the audience. If everyone already knows the basic folk tale, myth, or history that is being retold, no one wants the storyteller to tell it in an unadorned, linear fashion from A to B. The storyteller's contribution is considered to be the embellishments, the mirrors, the digressions, the analogies, the mappings onto political events, and so on. Thus, the real storytelling in fact happens in the nonlinearity, somewhere other than the origin point A or the destination point B.

In Hinduism, and in some traditions of Indigenous cultures from the Americas, the concept of time is not strictly linear. This can be reflected in the culture's religious beliefs and in linguistics. In Chinese cultures, the concept of time is similarly nonlinear, but for a particular historical reason called "dynastic cycle." Because China has a recorded history that extends so much further back than most written histories, patterns stretching back centuries or millennia become visible in a way impossible in shorter histories. One of the undeniable phenomena is the dynastic cycle. Throughout Chinese history, a dynasty will arise, ascend in power, and achieve a cultural, economic, political, and/or military pinnacle. Then, because of moral or political corruption, the dynasty will lose the "Mandate of Heaven" (i.e., the supernatural authority to rule) and inevitably decline until it is replaced by another dynasty. That dynasty then goes through the same cycle.

This idea of the circularity of time infects all aspects of Chinese cultures. Western countries largely come from a legalist tradition, which dictates that a just society is the product of the rule of law, not of the moral superiority of a particular leader. Legalist traditions tend to emphasize the written word as the clearest, least biased, truest representation of an idea. Nonlegalist traditions do things differently. In Chinese cultures, repetition is common. The reason for this is that new information is gained with each repetition.

Thus, when an American lawyer makes a business proposal on behalf of a client company, the lawyer expects to only have to make the proposal in person once, if at all. The written proposal speaks for itself better than any in-person presentation could. However, her Chinese counterparts might receive this very differently. They might ask her to fly to China to make the presentation personally. Then, that night, they might take her to dinner and expect her to make the proposal again. Then the next morning, they might take her to a traditional fried-cruller breakfast and ask her to make the proposal again. Then, they might take her golfing or to Shanghai Disneyland and expect her to make the proposal again.

The American lawyer is thinking, "Why do I have to repeat myself constantly? Aren't they listening? It's the same information every time."

Her Chinese counterparts would have a very different perception of these repeated recountings of the proposal. For them, the information is *not* the same every time. Each repetition might include the same words, but those words also come wrapped in new relational and emotional information. The Chinese counterparts might say, "I can't assess this proposal until I know more about the person making it."

For example, what if the language of the proposal said that one side could substitute an unavailable item with a "reasonable substitute" or could temporarily delay performance for "reasonable cause"? What constitutes "reasonable"? No contract could possibly lay out every potential situation and dictate ahead of time what would be reasonable in each situation.

The Chinese counterparts could understandably think, "It's impossible to know what this contract really says because it's impossible to know what this person thinks is reasonable, and it is impossible to know that because we don't know this person. Thus, we need to get to know this person and have a relationship with this person before we can judge what this proposal means. For example, is this a patient person? Is this a respectful person? We've treated her to dinner, traditional fried-cruller breakfast, and Shanghai Disneyland. And she seems to be getting impatient and eager to race back home. This tells us that this is a person who thinks in the short term, who is unwilling to learn about how business is done in China, who chooses to view things through her own eyes alone, and who thinks of herself first. This is a typical American."

I was born in Taiwan, raised in the United States, and have worked with many Chinese clients as both an attorney and an art dealer. I can attest, from firsthand experience, to the existence of this cultural chasm in business styles. And I've learned that repetition is one of the critical differences.

Let's examine the values of the story "Spring, Summer, Asteroid, Bird" and why it is told as a circular narrative. As previously discussed, the story visits the same characters (Chelsea and Marilyn) and the same location (fig tree in Southern Montana) multiple times. The revisiting of these elements evinces how no single, individual account can capture truth as fully as the community of multiple passes over the same elements, as stated previously. However, there is a further layer of analysis. Circular and nested structures often reveal themselves, upon extended contemplation, to contain a much larger emotional or spiritual component. That component might be quite spectral in nature but is often the most important truth of all.

In this story, the fact that Chelsea and Marilyn are cousins is mentioned repeatedly. In fact, birds are part of the theropod lineup of dinosaurs, as were A-listers such as *Tyrannosaurus rex*, *Velociraptor*, and *Allosaurus*. We, as Westerners trained to scan stories for tension, conflict, and the resolution thereof, might see this as a tale of catty female rivalry, with the underdog winning out. Hence, we would read Chelsea's hypothetical, impossible smile at the end as snark. However, an East Asian person reading the story might see it very differently. The emphasis on the fact that Chelsea and Marilyn are distant cousins means that their family survives. Even after dire, planet-ending calamity hits them, one of them continues on, which means their family continues on. And that is reason to smile.

There is a Zen parable that is apt here, the parable of the waterfall. A river travels its course as one body of water, united, indivisible. This is the cosmic whole from which we originate.

The river then meets the edge of a cliff and tumbles over. This is analogous to being born. As the water falls through the air, it divides into individual drops of water. Each drop is unique; no two drops are alike in shape, size, position, or path to the same destination. The length of the fall is the span of a life. We live our lives thinking we are individuals, each unique and irreplaceable.

Then the drops hit the bottom and rejoin each other as one river. They become a single wholeness again. We must not mourn that merging as the loss of our individuality, which was just a temporary separation and an illusion of uniqueness. We must think of the rejoining as each drop gaining back the rest of the river.

This is the sort of mist of values that drapes over the circular and nested structures. It is subtle, often a philosophical, spiritual, or emotional element, and sometimes very moving. Let us turn now to some masterful case studies demonstrating this.

HERO

An example of a circular story with this larger mist of values is
the movie *Hero*, an acclaimed 2002 Chinese martial arts epic
written and directed by Zhang Yimou, who is known for directing
Raise the Red Lantern, among other films, and for directing the opening and closing ceremonies of the 2008 Beijing Olympics (which gets
my vote for greatest live performance in human history). *Hero* applies
the *Rashomon* structure but goes one step further. It adds bold color
schemes to differentiate the sections. Spoilers ahoy, but actually, circular and nested stories are by design harder to spoil. So even if you
haven't seen it, reading the following summary will not significantly
deprive you of important pleasures.

Thousands of years ago, what we now call China was divided into
seven warring kingdoms. The story takes place in the middle of that
conflict.

Qin is the king of one of the kingdoms. He seeks to conquer the other
kingdoms in order to unite them into one vast empire.

The other kingdoms consider Qin a tyrant, especially because he
promises to not just conquer the other kingdoms but to destroy their
cultures, including their languages and writing systems. Thus, the other
kingdoms constantly send assassins to try to kill Qin.

Qin most fears the assassins from the kingdom of Zhao. The three
most formidable assassins are named Sky, Broken Sword, and Flying Snow. One day, one of Qin's magistrates, referred to as Nameless,

enters the palace, claiming that he has defeated all three of the assassins from Zhao.

As evidence of his defeat of Sky, Nameless presents to the king Sky's spear. The king tells Nameless that he hasn't permitted anyone to approach within one hundred paces of his person since the last assassination attempt. However, Qin allows Nameless the great honor of approaching within twenty paces of the king to share a drink, in gratitude for his defeating Sky.

Nameless then proceeds to tell the king how he challenged Sky to a duel in front of the king's own men and killed Sky. We see this duel enacted as if we are ourselves witnesses to its truth.

Nameless then presents to Qin the swords of Broken Sword and Flying Snow. Nameless tells the king that Broken Sword and Flying Snow were lovers, and that Nameless cleverly used the jealousy between them over Broken Sword's pretty assistant to defeat them both. As reward, the king permits Nameless to approach even closer, within ten paces.

Nameless tells the king about how he defeated Broken Sword and Flying Snow. In a flashback sequence that is coded with a red color scheme, we see that Broken Sword and Flying Snow were torn apart by disagreement, resentment, and jealousy. Broken Sword bedded his young assistant, and in revenge, Flying Snow killed Broken Sword. Nameless claims that he seized upon Flying Snow's guilt over killing her lover to challenge her to a duel and then killed her in front of the king's men.

We return to the meeting between Qin and Nameless. The king announces that he does not believe what Nameless says, because he knows that Broken Sword and Flying Snow are not that immature. The king explains that he knows this because he battled them himself, and in the course of battling them, learned enough about them to admire them.

The king tells Nameless what he thinks actually happened. The king surmises that Nameless is an assassin and that he colluded with Broken Sword and Flying Snow. We then see enacted a conjectural sequence coded with a blue color scheme. We see that the two lovers agreed to allow Nameless to kill them and decided that they would stage a fight in front of the king's men. The king guesses that they did this with the specific goal of getting Nameless within ten paces of the king, because Nameless must be master of some martial arts move that is deadly but requires proximity to the victim.

Nameless admits that the king is very astute. Nameless confesses that he is actually an orphan from the kingdom of Zhao and that he has been seeking revenge against the king because the king's men killed Nameless's family.

Nameless tells the king about their plan. We then witness a confessional sequence coded with a white color scheme. In it, we see that Nameless perfected a sword move that allowed him to pierce an opponent but miss vital organs. He, Sky, Broken Sword, and Flying Snow conspired to use this unusual skill in front of the king's men to fool them into thinking that Nameless killed the assassins. The goal was in fact to get Nameless close enough to the king to perform another assassination technique.

However, Nameless claims that Broken Sword had a change of heart. Nameless says that Broken Sword pleaded with Nameless to spare the king because Broken Sword had come to believe that it would be better for all the people in the various kingdoms for Qin to defeat them if it would mean the end of war. Broken Sword believed that the destruction of the other kingdoms' cultures was not as costly a price as the loss of lives from continuing to war.

The king then points out that Nameless has no weapon, since all visitors are thoroughly searched before being allowed in the king's chambers. How does Nameless plan to assassinate the king? Nameless says he planned to do so by seizing the king's own sword and using it against him. The king sees that he has been outmaneuvered and outmatched, at least in combat skill. He willingly throws his sword to Nameless.

The king then tells Nameless of the last time he battled Broken Sword and Flying Snow, in a flashback sequence coded with a green color scheme. The assassins broke into his palace and fought skillfully, cutting down hundreds of the king's guards. While Flying Snow fended off the guards and prevented them from entering the king's hall to protect him, Broken Sword was to hunt down the king and finish him off. However, at the last moment, Broken Sword relented and spared the king, which enraged Flying Snow.

The king wonders if it is possible that Broken Sword spared him for the reason Nameless gave. Can it be that the king's own enemy understands that his purpose in conquering the other kingdoms is to save lives? The king has been called a tyrant because he wants to destroy the cultures of the other kingdoms. However, the king sees that multiplicity breeds war. When people are divided by different languages, different writing systems, different values, they invariably turn difference into hatred, which leads to bloodshed. The only answer that the king sees to this is the elimination of difference. The choice is that or loss of life. The king marvels that his enemy Broken Sword understands his intent enough to lay down his own sword.

Nameless then flies toward the king and performs his assassination technique. However, at the last moment, he curbs his blow and spares the king's life. He asks that when the king finally conquers their other cultures, he remember that the goal of swordsmanship (as a metaphor for violence and force) is ultimately peace.

The king's archers encircle Nameless but the king hesitates in issuing the order for them to let their arrows fly. The king's ministers implore him to issue the order since Nameless attempted to assassinate the king, and if the king seeks orderly rule, he cannot let such an act go unpunished.

The king is thrust into an agonizing and impossible decision. He is being forced to kill a good and brave man, a hero. This man is his enemy, but this man understands him in a way that so few people do. This man understands that the king does not wish to do this but that he does this for the greater good and that a true leader often has to make decisions that no one else wants to make. This man understands and gives the king his blessing and is willing to sacrifice his own life for the very peace that the king himself wants.

The king orders the archers to shoot. The sky darkens with arrows as they fly toward Nameless. The scene ends with a gate bristling with thousands of arrows except for a shape in the form of a man. Nonetheless, although Nameless is executed as an assassin, the king orders that he be buried as a hero. The king and Nameless both understood that in every war, there are heroes on both sides.

Hero offers some clear, practical takeaways for storytellers. Circular stories create plot opportunities for reversals, twists, and subterfuge. Circular stories also allow opportunities to chart how characters change their minds and evolve in their understanding of the world. However, in order to fully appreciate how the values behind *Hero* dictate that it be told in this circular structure, we need to understand the controversy behind it.

For much of his career, director Zhang Yimou found himself battling Chinese censors over a number of elements in his films. Some of them were not political (sex scenes), some of them were political (showing China in an unflattering and feudal light to world audiences). *Hero* was a departure for him. It was criticized by some reviewers as being propaganda for Chinese imperialism. Many viewers saw parallels between Qin's desire to conquer other kingdoms, despite their cultures being very different, and China's seizing of places as diverse and as culturally, politically, religiously, and ethnically different from the rest of China as Tibet, Hong Kong, and Xinjiang. Of course, Taiwan and China's claims over it is another resonance.

The film has insurrectionists from these smaller kingdoms willingly abandoning their cause and their independence because they acknowledge that being absorbed into the larger empire represents the greater overall good. This is viewed by some as wish fulfillment for the Chinese government. Further, the film has Nameless agree to sacrifice his life and his culture, but the victor has a moral obligation as well. The king must honor the cultures he destroys after he has destroyed them. The king is depicted as an honorable man, and he honors Nameless as a hero after destroying him and his culture.

The reliability of an empire's promises to remember and honor those it vanquishes has a pretty miserable history. Critics scoffed at the idea that Qin would honor those it defeated. They criticized Zhang Yimou as a tool of the Chinese government and viewed his film as propaganda for the empty promises China makes to the cultures it absorbs. They pointed to how China promised to honor Hong Kong's very different and democratic culture via a "one country, two systems" approach and how quickly and spectacularly China incinerated those promises.

But Zhang Yimou is an artist. What he does with *Hero* is far more sophisticated than the political arguments from either the Chinese government or its critics. The film explores the idea of whether diversity is a negative force because multiplicity creates chaos. The king of Qin laments that the different systems of weights and measurements hinder trade between the countries. He sees a tumble of kingdoms that are riven by the multiplicity of languages and writing systems, which prevent people from communicating efficiently with each other. Further, the differences give them incentives to identify on a smaller, more tribal, more clannish level, rather than seeing the commonality among all the people in the kingdoms. That tribalism leads to war and death. Qin thus sees multiplicity or diversity as an evil to be eradicated.

The multiplicity of competing versions of the events that we see enacted in differently colored sections of the film serves as a metaphor for the multiplicity that the king seeks to unify under one culture. The multiplicity of versions of events creates chaos and confusion in the mind of the viewer, just like the multiplicity of cultures creates chaos and war in the seven kingdoms.

However, Zhang Yimou subverts the idea that this multiplicity is a wholly negative thing, even if it does result in chaos. It is the chaos that draws us deeper into the important moral questions in the film. The multiplicity of mutually exclusive accounts alerts us that one or more of the narrators is unreliable. This sets up a mystery structure that impels the viewer to investigate the story more deeply. The process of trying to solve the puzzle leads the viewer to explore the motivations for the unreliable narration, which in turn leads to a reveal about the internal conflicts in the two main narrators. The accounts are conflicting, just like the narrators' hearts are conflicted. A simpler, more linear narrative with characters who agonize less about their moral dilemmas would be both less artful and less true.

Further, Zhang Yimou manages to do exactly what Nameless urges the king to do: honor those who are defeated. The most memorable passage in the film is the red sequence. It takes place in a calligraphy school in the deserts of the kingdom of Zhao. The school is a pavilion painted a striking red, in the middle of a featureless sandy plain.

Nameless has tracked down Broken Sword and Flying Snow there. The students at the calligraphy school practice the Zhao language under their wizened master. Outside, the armies of Qin amass. Thousands of soldiers and archers gather outside the school. One chilling touch is that the extras hired to portray the army were actual soldiers of the People's Liberation Army, the very army that would invade Taiwan or implement crackdowns on Hong Kong or Xinjiang.

The soldiers launch thousands of arrows at the school. They are able to penetrate through the walls and ceilings. The students flee as arrows stab into their hall. However, their master does not flee. He instead takes his customary seat at the head of the classroom. If he is going to die, he is going to die practicing his culture.

The students are moved by his courage and his final act of resistance. They return to their seats. Even as students are pierced by arrows, their surviving classmates continue practicing the Zhao language as long as they live.

We ultimately learn that this red-encoded section never happened. It was all a ruse. Nonetheless, the film does something fascinating. Even after we learn the "true" version of events, that is, the white and green sections, the beauty and purpose of the other versions remain. In fact, it is clear that Zhang Yimou heavily stacked the sections that are ultimately shown to be "lies," like that red section, with the most astonishing and moving images in the whole film.

The subtext is that all those other versions helped us to arrive at the ending, with the deep understanding between the conquered Nameless and his conqueror, the king. The fact that the red section and various other sections were disproved and "vanquished" by the "true" sections doesn't erase them. In fact, it is those "conquered" sections that people remember most often. Zhang Yimou has thus done exactly what Nameless pleaded with the king to do: honor the victor's obligation to remember and uplift those it conquers.

Regardless of whether it's fair to see in *Hero* a metaphor for China's absorption of various cultures, Zhang Yimou provides an example of the nobleness of honoring this moral obligation in his art. The film uses the multiplicity of the various accounts in the circular story structure to carry the themes it explores. There is thus a synthesis between the values the film explores and the structure of the film. Substance and form are in harmony with each other. The result is a mist of resonance over the film that elevates it into true artistry.

THE THOUSAND AND ONE NIGHTS

At last, we arrive at the most famous of all nonlinear Eastern stories, *The Thousand and One Nights*. The book is an anonymously written collection of nested tales that are probably from the Muslim world, Persia, India, and China, organized by a frame tale. There are many versions, with different tales and different organizations of tales, beginning with eighth-century Arabic translations of a Persian text. One of the most well-known English versions is a nineteenth-century translation by Sir Richard Burton. Note that any modern recommendation of *The Thousand and One Nights* should be accompanied by a content warning for racism, sexism, sexual violence, and animal cruelty.

The Thousand and One Nights is known for both the inventiveness of its component tales and for its dizzying nested structure of tales within tales.

Frame Tale of Shahrazad (aka Sheherazade or Scheherazade) (First Level)

Shahriyar, the king of India and China, discovers his wife's infidelity. He kills her and then vows that he will repeatedly wed a new woman only to kill her the morning after their wedding night so that she can never betray him like his queen did. The king's vizier has a brave daughter named Shahrazad. The Burton translation (adapted by Jack Zipes) describes her as being extremely learned, having read and collected one thousand books of history, and having a knowledge of poetry, philosophy, the sciences, and the arts. She is described as wise, witty, pleasant, and polite.

Remarkably, there is no mention of Shahrazad's physical appearance in her introduction, just a long list of her various intellectual achievements and character virtues. Shahrazad develops a plan to stop the king and save the realm's women from being wedded and beheaded. She convinces her father to offer her as bride to the king. Then, on their wedding night, she begins telling him one enchanting, interconnected tale after another, only to stop at dawn on a cliffhanger, ensuring that the king will allow her to live to the next night so he can hear what happens next.

"The Tale of the Fisherman and the Jinnee" (Second Level)

In Shahrazad's first tale, a fisherman lets a djinni (or jinnee) out of a bottle. The djinni, embittered at being imprisoned, has vowed to kill whoever sets him free, but as reward, he will allow the person to name the manner of his death. The fisherman feigns disbelief that the djinni could have fit in the bottle. He says he won't believe it unless the djinni demonstrates it. The boastful djinni puts himself back in the bottle and the fisherman seals him within it again. The fisherman excoriates the djinni for his ingratitude at the fisherman's setting him free and compares their tale to the story of King Yunan and the sage Duban, which he proceeds to tell the djinni.

"The Tale of King Yunan and the Sage Duban" (Third Level)

Physician Duban cures King Yunan of his leprosy. The king showers riches and honors on Duban in gratitude. The king's vizier grows jealous and spreads lies to the king, trying to convince him that Duban is an assassin sent to kill him. The king accuses the vizier of telling lies out of envy and says that if he were to punish Duban like the vizier urges, he would be no better than the man in the story of the husband and the parrot, which he proceeds to tell the vizier.

"The Tale of the Husband and the Parrot" (Fourth Level)

A jealous man brings a parrot to spy on his wife while he is gone and to report back about what happens in his absence. The parrot reports that he saw the man's wife with a lover. The man beats his wife. The wife then uses sprinkled water, noise makers, and mirrors to delude the bird into thinking there is a storm outside. The next time the parrot reports to the man that there was a storm, when the man knows there was no storm, he assumes that the parrot is foolish and told him falsehoods, and that his wife is innocent of adultery, and he kills the parrot. When the man discovers for himself the truth of his wife's adultery, he kills both the wife and her lover and mourns the death of the wrongfully accused parrot.

"The Tale of King Yunan and the Sage Duban" continued (Third Level)

Upon hearing the tale of the husband and the parrot, King Yunan's vizier proclaims his innocence and says that if what he said about the physician Duban is not true, the king should strike him down, like the dissolute vizier in the tale of the prince and the ogress, which he proceeds to recount.

"The Tale of the Prince and the Ogress" (Fourth Level)

A king entrusts his vizier to take the king's son on a hunting trip. The vizier encourages the young prince to wander off alone. The young prince gets lost and is almost eaten by an ogress, escaping only with the help of prayers to God. As punishment, the king slays his vizier.

"The Tale of King Yunan and the Sage Duban" continued (Third Level)

The weak-willed King Yunan believes his vizier and sentences Duban to beheading. Duban is resigned to his fate but tells the king that after cutting off his head, the king should place it on a jar, then turn to a particular page of a special book that Duban will provide, and his severed head will answer any question the king asks. The king, desiring to see such a wonder, agrees. After Duban is beheaded and the head placed upon a jar, the king begins turning the pages of the book. However, the pages are stuck, so the king moistens his fingers with his tongue to turn the pages. The king shortly goes into convulsions and dies, for Duban poisoned the pages and the king ingested the poison upon moistening his fingers.

"The Tale of the Fisherman and the Jinnee" continued (Second Level)

The fisherman says that the djinni received his rightful reward for his ingratitude, just like the ungrateful King Yunan. The djinni swears that if the fisherman lets him out of the bottle again, he will not kill the fisherman. The fisherman says that he is giving the djinni exactly what he deserves. The djinni begs for mercy, even though undeserved, and promises to show the fisherman how to become wealthy. The fisherman agrees. The djinni takes the fisherman to a special pond where he can catch enchanted fish to sell to the sultan for a high price. The fisherman sells the enchanted fish to the sultan. When the sultan's cook cooks them, a mysterious visitor magically appears through the walls and speaks to the fish, who answer back. The sultan decides to go searching for the cause of such wonders. While searching, he discovers an abandoned palace, inside of which is a young king who has been turned half into marble. The king tells the sultan the story of how that happened.

"The Tale of the Enchanted King" (Third Level)

The young king explains that he was cursed by his queen, who is an enchantress. The young king learned that his wife had taken a lover. He struck down the lover. In revenge, his queen turned the young king half into marble.

"The Tale of the Fisherman and the Jinnee" continued (Second Level)

The sultan, enraged by this injustice, tricks the queen into turning the young king back into a man and kills the woman. In gratitude, the young king pledges his loyalty to the sultan and agrees to let the sonless sultan adopt him as his son. The sultan also bestows rewards on the fisherman for bringing him the fish that eventually led to the discovery of his new son. Thus, in this circle of nested tales, loyalty is justly rewarded, the perfidy of djinni and women are punished, and patriarchy is upheld (or so it seems on initial analysis).

Frame Tale of Shahrazad (First Level)

After telling tales like the ones we just examined for 1,001 consecutive nights and bearing King Shahriyar children over their years together, Shahrazad begs the king to renounce his vow to wed and behead the women of the realm and implores him to return to his senses. He agrees. Thus, through her courage and ingenuity and the power of storytelling, Shahrazad saves herself and the women of the realm.

On the most superficial level, *The Thousand and One Nights* is about themes of loyalty, betrayal, justice, and revenge, which it revisits over and over. Many of the tales are about the treachery of women, djinni, and slaves. The nested structure seems designed to repeatedly return to these morality themes as a way to elevate the moral lesson from a specific relationship between particular characters to higher and more universal truths.

However, nested within that is a deeper level of meaning. The nesting of the tales and their ingenious structure is concerned less with any substantive themes than with demonstrating the dazzling power of storytelling. The power of storytelling is at the heart of the frame tale. Thus, it is a story whose substance is putatively and superficially about certain moral themes (loyalty, betrayal, justice) but whose form is about the power of story itself.

However, nested within *that* is an even deeper tale that utilizes the relational nature of the nested structure. One main strength of this storytelling form is that it emphasizes the discovery of relationships among the individual units within the greater work. Even though the book predates modern notions of mental health by over a thousand years, I read that deeper relationship tale buried in *The Thousand and One Nights* as an attempt to address a mental health crisis with empathy.

King Shahriyar was so broken by his wife's betrayal that he suffered acute mental distress and did a horrendous thing. While his actions might be read as sociopathic, they were probably unsurprising given his power and the century and world in which he lived.

Shahrazad has the empathy to understand that the king had suffered this acute mental distress, and to realize that her harrowing mission is actually a mission to bring the king back to his senses, back to himself. However, she enters the task without preconceived moral judgment of the king. She instinctively realizes that she needs to meet the king where he is mentally and emotionally, which is, at the beginning of the story, in a very dark state.

Thus, she spins him tale after tale that echoes his own sense of betrayal, a betrayal that led to this current wretched state. It's as if she were saying, "I know how you feel. I know how hurt you were." She's accepted that healing and wellness are slow processes and that she must be patient. So for nearly three years, she spends every night building a connection with the King to let him know that she understands and empathizes with how he must feel.

Further, she doesn't just tell him this, she shows him through stories, because stories reach us in ways that nothing else can. She instinctively senses that words of agreement would bounce off of him in his state. Only the power of story would be able to show him that she feels his pain.

However, she doesn't want to just humor and coddle him. She doesn't want to just feed him sweet opiates that keep him comfortably stewing in his sense of having been wronged. Thus, she weens him off the milk by injecting drops of vinegar into the mixture. She seeds in tales about tyrannical and unjust leaders who abuse their powers or fail to show mercy.

The juxtaposition of those stories against the stories of betrayal draws an unspoken analogy between the villains the king despises and himself. The subtext is, "King, you are through your actions betraying your people, betraying justice, betraying your better self. King, you are in danger of becoming what you hate."

The development of this relationship isn't linear. It doesn't rise conveniently to fit a tidy structure or schedule. It is messy and irregular and goes in fits and starts, full of setbacks and repeated retreats backward and steps forward, just like real healing and recovery.

Then, finally, at the end of nearly three years, after having borne the king multiple children, she calls upon him to reverse his decree. She calls upon him to return to his senses. She calls upon him to return to his true self. Thus, *The Thousand and One Nights*, for all its salacious material and treacherous characters and seemingly objectionable themes, is ultimately a story about how patience and empathy can reach even the most lost souls and give them their true selves back. It is also an exploration of how stories do that better than anything else because stories are empathy engines.

None of this would have been possible without the nested structure. The structure allows Shahrazad to develop a relationship with the king, which allows him to believe in her empathy and really hear her stories. This allows the king to develop a relationship with the stories of wronged men, stories that he feels capture his own feelings and in which he sees himself. Then Shahrazad invites the king to have a relationship with the stories of tyrants that show him what he is in danger of becoming and what he doesn't want to see, which would have been impossible with a simpler, more linear structure. The repetition creates the trust between Shahrazad and the king, which allows for the relationship that the king develops with the stories, which allows the king to return to his own truer, better self. No individual tale could have accomplished that as effectively as this richer, more varied, more realistically diverse community of tales.

Thus, layers buried deep within *The Thousand and One Nights* show us that the epic is a moving testament to the importance of empathy, particularly in the face of a mental health crisis; the power of storytelling; and the depth of connection between people and stories. None of this would have been nearly as powerful were it not for the book's nested structure.

Closing Bows

Here we arrive at the end of our tale. In keeping with Eastern storytelling tradition, I end it abruptly to leave you in contemplation within the void of its sudden absence. May the ringing silence after its hasty departure beckon you on a journey to discover new stories.

We talk a lot about how diversity is beautiful, but less often about how beauty is diverse. This book is my attempt to start that conversation. The work to find room in our minds to accommodate new forms of beauty is nourishing and delicious and one of the great pleasures of having a mind. The ability to learn a new story, or a new kind of story, is a fundamental life experience.

A dinosaur named Chelsea used to tell herself a story that her cousin Marilyn was greater than Chelsea.

A dinosaur named Marilyn used to tell herself a story that her cousin Chelsea was meeker than Marilyn.

An asteroid slammed into their planet and ended the stories of most dinosaurs.

A dinosaur named Chelsea inherited that planet and started a new story.

May you have found play or discovery in the ideas in this story.

May you find delight in the notion that a story can surprise you with new ideas in the second half of its life.

May you discern higher patterns of truth in the repetition of elements in a story.

May you realize that the world is always full of new wonders for those who meet it with an open mind and a welcoming heart.

I invite storytellers to give themselves permission to learn about story forms from outside their own cultural tradition, in addition to including diverse characters.

I bid the gatekeepers of Western publishing to open their minds about what a satisfying story can look like.

I urge readers to swim just far enough out so that their feet can't touch bottom. I promise that the water is fine.

The world is a limitless place. Our understanding of it can be vast, varied, and venturous, or it can be simple, static, and safe. The choice is ours.

Appendix: Activities

As both an author and a writing instructor, I'm a fan of learning by doing. A stream of pretty abstractions delivered in lecture format often results in very fleeting retention of concepts. There's nothing like having to do exercises that test your understanding of an idea to tattoo it permanently onto your brain.

Thus, I've included some proposed exercises here, for both readers and writers. (Here I am using "readers" as a shorthand for consumers of stories in any medium, whether film or books or video games.) I would suggest that writers also do the section for readers, since writers are also readers. You can do them alone or as part of a class, book club, or writing group. You can read the book in its entirety and then do all the exercises, or you can read one of the four acts of the book and then do the exercises pertaining to that section. You can treat them as a trivia quiz or a drinking game or as meditative prompts. Use them as a liturgy around which to build a fictitious religion. Discuss ways they make you feel uncomfortable with your therapist or with an AI bot. Scratch your responses to them into the stone of your prison wall to pass the days. Fall back on them as cocktail party small talk to fill painful lulls in the conversation. In short, use them in any way you see fit. In true Eastern fashion, I relinquish will and intention over how you use them. They are yours to make your own.

QUESTIONS FOR READERS

ACT ONE—The East Asian Four-Act Story Structure

1. In "The Daughters of Itoya," what was your initial reaction to the act three introduction of warriors, bows and arrows, and killing? Did it intrigue you or irritate you? Why?

2. In *Parasite*, what was your initial reaction to the act three introduction of someone even poorer than the Kims? Did it draw you into the story further or push you away? With which characters did your sympathies lie after this reveal?

3. In the *Mario* and *Zelda* games, would you have noticed the four-act structure if you were watching children play these games? Why or why not?

4. How would you describe *Hard-Boiled Wonderland and the End of the World* to another reader in terms of genre and tone?

5. In *Your Name*, Mitsuha and Taki seem to be separated by distance, then time, then death. Did your reactions to the film change in tone as you continued watching?

ACT TWO—Circular/Nested Story Structures

1. In *Rashomon*, which of the four accounts of the crime do you believe the most and why?

2. In *The Merchant and the Alchemist's Gate*, do you feel that the characters have meaningful free will in determining their own fates? Why or why not?

3. How would your emotional reaction to *Everything Everywhere All at Once* differ if this were a realistic family drama where different life paths were referred to as conjectural abstracts rather than shown as other universes?

4. In the *Metroid* games, does revisiting the same areas repeatedly sound tedious or intriguing? Why?

ACT THREE—People Aren't People

1. Is there a story you think would be received similarly by most people regardless of their cultural background? What is that story?

2. Have you ever been annoyed by a tourist for violating a social custom in your culture? What was the custom?

3. Have you yourself ever violated a social custom as a tourist? What was the custom?

4. Which do you value more, being special or being good? Why?

5. What was the first work of art that made you interested in another culture? Have you gone back to revisit that work recently? Has your opinion of the work changed and, if so, how? Has your opinion of the culture changed and, if so, how?

ACT FOUR—Values Dictate Structures

1. List your top three most important values. How aware are other people that these values are important to you? Do you live these values and, if so, is that apparent to others or is it internal and invisible?

2. What is your favorite book, film, or video game? Does it reflect any of those values? If so, how?

3. Is there a book, film, or video game that seems to contradict your values that you nonetheless love? What is it and why do you love it? Can you identify its structure, form, or style?

4. Imagine you work for an American movie studio adapting *My Neighbor Totoro*. What changes would you make to it? Why would you make them? How would they change the spirit of the story?

5. Imagine you work for an American movie studio adapting *Hero*. What changes would you make to it? Who is the hero of the new adaptation?

6. Imagine you work for an American movie studio adapting *The Thousand and One Nights*. How do you justify the inclusion of tales that exhibit sexism, racism, or violence?

QUESTIONS FOR WRITERS

ACT ONE—The East Asian Four-Act Story Structure

1. In *Parasite*, how did the filmmaker make the elements in acts one and two more compelling to compensate for holding back the new act three element?

2. In the *Mario* and *Zelda* games, how central is the task of figuring out new rules throughout acts one and two?

3. In *Hard-Boiled Wonderland and the End of the World*, did you assume that the HBW and EOW strands of the book introduced in acts one and two would merge? Did you predict how they would merge?

4. In *Your Name*, what is gained or lost by having Mitsuha and Taki communicate in the first two acts only through brief phone messages and words written on their hands?

5. Identify the main story elements in your current work in progress. What element could you hold back as an act three surprise? How would that affect your story?

6. How would you raise the bar on your storytelling in acts one and two to compensate for the absence of the surprise element introduced in the latter half of the story?

7. What unseen relationships among all the elements in your story could be unveiled in act four?

ACT TWO — Circular/Nested Story Structures

1. Take a pivotal event in your story, either an event you have already written or one you are contemplating writing, and try the following:
   - Write a brief (one- to two-paragraph) description of the event from the point of view of your main character.
   - Write a brief description of the event from the point of view of your main antagonist or secondary character.
   - Write a brief description of the event from the point of view of your main character thinking back on the event many years later.
   - Write a brief description of the event from the point of view of your main antagonist or secondary character thinking back on the event many years later.
   - Write a brief description of the event from the point of view of your main character anticipating or conjecturing about the event many years beforehand.
   - Write a brief description of the event from the point of view of your main antagonist or secondary character anticipating or conjecturing about the event many years beforehand.

2. What is the device that unites these various descriptions of the same event in your story?
   - Competing versions that are mutually incompatible (*Rashomon*)?
   - Repeated recountings that reveal additional layers, onion-style (*Hero*)?
   - Nested tales riffing on the same theme (*The Thousand and One Nights*)?
   - Nested tales that interact with each other (*The Merchant and the Alchemist's Gate*)?
   - Emotional/physical trauma (*Last Year at Marienbad*)?

3. How do the various descriptions of the events differ?

4. What do the changes in those descriptions say about the characters' arcs over the years?

5. What is the most intuitive order for the reader to read those descriptions?

6. What is the least intuitive order for the reader to read those descriptions?

7. What can be gained in departing from the most intuitive order in terms of the following story elements?
- Plot twists/surprises
- Tension
- Emotional contrast
- Thematic power

8. Even if you don't plan on structuring your entire book in a cyclic or nested form, how can you use this exercise to enrich your story? In other words, how can you fracture the depiction of this one pivotal event and seed those shards throughout the book to add richness to your book as a whole?

ACT THREE—People Aren't People

1. What are you proudest of?

2. What is the dark side of what you are proudest of?

3. What are you most ashamed of?

4. What is the bright side of what you are most ashamed of?

5. Whom do you find most deplorable?

6. What do you have in common with that person?

7. What is the greatest compliment a loved one has ever paid you?

8. What is the greatest compliment a stranger has ever paid you?

9. What aspect of yourself would you most like someone to compliment you on that no one has ever mentioned?

10. You have twenty-four hours to live. What would you say and to whom?

11. You have twenty-four hours to live, but one quote of yours will become famous around the world for five hundred years. What would the quote be? How do you fear that quote might be misinterpreted?

ACT FOUR—Values Dictate Structures

1. Which act structure would fit your story the best? Why?

2. Which act structure would fit your story the worst? Why?

3. What effects could be squeezed out of your story by trying to cram it into the worst-fitting structure?

4. How many movements would your story be if it were a symphony or some other piece of classical music? Why?

5. Would your story be better adapted as a film or television series? Why?

6. If your story were adapted as a television series, how long would each episode be? Why?

7. If your story were adapted as a television series, how many episodes would there be in season one? Why? How many seasons would there be? Why?

8. Imagine your story as a city skyline or mountain range. Draw its silhouette. Then count the number of mountains or skyscrapers in it.

9. Imagine your story as a house. Draw its footprint, indicating size and shape of rooms, their functions, and the pathways among them.

10. What are the tentpole (i.e., most important) scenes in your story?

How many are there? Where do they occur? Are they distributed evenly throughout the story or not? Why or why not?

11. Identify a way that you self-categorize. For example, by astrological sign, generational identity, Chinese zodiacal sign, Myers-Briggs personality type, and so on. Then identify the type in that system that is most polar to your personality. What structure would your opposite personality type choose to tell your story?

12. Describe your story in three brief sentences and time how long it takes you to write those sentences. Then describe your story in four brief sentences and time how long it takes you to write those sentences. What accounts for the difference?

13. Describe your story in three words. Then describe your story in four words. Which set of words would you prefer to wear on your clothing or book merch apparel, as a tattoo, or as some other personal adornment?

14. Imagine your story as a person. Design your story's tombstone, but not the words on it, only the nonverbal elements. What is its shape, size, and design?

ACKNOWLEDGMENTS

I bow to my agents Alex Slater and Will Watkins and my editor Claire Wallace, as well as project editor Dassi Zeidel, copyeditor Rebecca Rider, project manager Louise Mattarelliano, managing editor Becky Homiski, associate art director Derek Thornton, psychotherapist/LMFT James McLindon, and all the institutions that let me teach and publish the material that became this book and never once asked me to lower my freak flag: UCLA, Writing the Other, SFWA, Clarion West, Rambo Academy, University of Iowa, SCBWI, CBWLA, NCTE, Lighthouse Writers Workshop, Selecky Writing School, Margins Conference, New England Writers' Center, and Hydra House Books.

NOTES

1. Michael Paulson, "'Hamilton' Is Coming to the Small Screen. This Is How It Got There," *New York Times*, June 25, 2020.
2. Carl Jung, *The Portable Jung*, ed. Joseph Campbell, trans. R.F.C. Hull (Penguin Classics, 1976), 320–21.
3. Robert Colvile, "Spot the WEIRDo," *Aeon*, July 20, 2016.
4. Colvile, "Spot the WEIRDo."
5. James McLindon, email message to author, May 2024.
6. Laurel Thatcher Ulrich, *Well-Behaved Women Seldom Make History* (Knopf, 2007), xiii–xvi.
7. K. S. Yang and L. Lu, eds., *Chinese Self: Psychology Analysis* (Chongqing University Press, 2009), quoted in Weijun Ma et al., "Toward the Theoretical Constructs of East Asian Cultural Psychology," in *Unity, Diversity and Culture, Proceedings from the 22nd Congress of the International Association for Cross-Cultural Psychology*, ed. Christine Roland-Lévy et al. (International Association for Cross-Cultural Psychology, 2016), 91.
8. Ravi Chandra, "Director Daniel Kwan: 'Genius Emerges from the Collective,'" *Psychology Today*, March 13, 2023.
9. Daniel Kwan, Academy Awards acceptance speech, Dolby Theatre, Hollywood, CA, March 12, 2023.
10. Lev Grossman, "Top 10 Novels of the 2000s," *Time*, January 8, 2010.
11. Salman Rushdie, interview by Harriett Gilbert, *World Book Club*, BBC, October 1, 2005.